PRAISE FOR

JESUS UNFORSAKEN

"After so many centuries of transactional, retributive theology and the propagation of toxic images of God, the temptation of so many post-moderns who bear the wounds of religious PTSD is to oversteer wildly into oncoming traffic. Said plainly, healthy deconstruction has devolved into simply expunging Jesus from spirituality. They'd rather be bereft of faith than continue in spiritual slavery.

Enter Keith Giles. Against the dominant flow of exiles toward a spiritual vacuum, Keith stubbornly anchors himself and his image of God in Jesus—the true and wounded God of the apostles. This Jesus reveals God as love and nothing else. How? In the way he ascends his Cross-shaped throne, exposes the myth of redemptive violence, and embodies God's freedom to forgive. If divine punishment is off the table, why did Jesus die? *Jesus Unforsaken* reveals a more beautiful, alternative vision."

— BRADLEY JERSAK, DEAN OF THEOLOGY & CULTURE, ST. STEPHEN'S UNIVERSITY (NEW BRUNSWICK) AND CO-AUTHOR OF *THE PASTOR: A CRISIS*

"If you want to understand the atonement outside the confining box of penal substitution, then this is the book for you."

— MATTHEW J. DISTEFANO, AUTHOR OF *FROM THE BLOOD OF ABEL* AND *HERETIC!*

PRAISE FOR THE

JESUS UN SERIES

"Those of the Church Fathers who espoused universal salvation were moved to do so not only from the conviction that this was the testimony of scripture, but also from the radical notion that, when we say that God is love or call him Father, we are not just spouting pious nonsense, but are saying something both logically coherent and necessarily true. Keith Giles has no purpose in these pages but to demonstrate how right they were."

— DAVID BENTLEY HART, AUTHOR OF *THAT ALL SHALL BE SAVED*

"Citing scripture, ancient Church leaders, and contemporary biblical scholars, Keith Giles makes a compelling case against hell. What makes this book especially winsome is the accessible way Giles writes. The conversation is easy to follow and arguments compelling. This book is both an encyclopedic resource and conversation starter!"

— THOMAS JAY OORD, AUTHOR OF *GOD CAN'T: HOW TO BELIEVE IN GOD AND LOVE AFTER TRAGEDY, ABUSE, AND OTHER EVILS* AND *THE UNCONTROLLING LOVE OF GOD*

"*Jesus Undefeated* reveals an early church corpus who, through their common sense and sacred intuition, knew what we moderns seem to have so inexplicably forgotten. They corporately knew God far too well to believe Him capable of ever creating such a bone-torturing Hell...This lie needs to fry. And Keith, as a master conceptual chef, does just that in his wonderful new book which I heartily recommend."

— RICHARD MURRAY, AUTHOR OF *GOD VERSUS EVIL: SCULPTING AN EPIC THEOLOGY OF GOD'S HEROIC GOODNESS* AND *THE QUESTION OF HELL*

"Keith, in a very readable fashion and conversational tone, reexamines the idea of the afterlife and demythologizes the concept of hell, all with a thorough application of the Bible, the Church Fathers, and theologians. But what I like most about his work is that it comes from a big heart motivated by love to include all. And isn't this the thrust of the gospel?"

— DAVID HAYWARD, THE NAKEDPASTOR

"Keith Giles has crafted a deeply helpful and valuable gift that would have saved me years."

— WM. PAUL YOUNG, AUTHOR OF *THE SHACK*

"Anyone who cares what the New Testament says about 'the End Times' owes it to themselves to read this insightful work."

— GREG BOYD, AUTHOR OF *THE MYTH OF A CHRISTIAN NATION*

"[Keith] draws our attention to something more captivatingly beautiful—the presence of Christ within us inviting us to participate in an adventure that is already happening."

— ANDRE RABE, AUTHOR, PUBLIC SPEAKER, PHILOSOPHER, AND RADICAL THEOLOGIAN

"[Jesus's] message, once so counter-cultural, has been stifled, suffocated, and reduced to a tangled pile of knots on the floor of the American political scene. I can think of no better place for a Christian to begin sorting those out, and reclaiming a message that is still other-worldly after all these years, than with *Jesus Untangled*."

— BENJAMIN L. COREY, AUTHOR OF *UNDILUTED: REDISCOVERING THE RADICAL MESSAGE OF JESUS*

"The best books about Jesus are the ones that are as challenging as they are inspiring and as entertaining as they are informative. Keith Giles nails it in *Jesus Untangled*. It's a book about love, and it's a love extended to all the different tribal factions that all-too-often fight for Christian supremacy at the expense of Christ's teachings."

— JOHN FUGELSANG, HOST OF "TELL ME EVERYTHING", SIRIUS XM RADIO

"Keith Giles runs with that company of Christ-followers committed to proclaiming that Jesus Christ is the Word of God, our final Authority for faith and practice...Fear not: Keith does not throw the Bible under the bus. But he will dethrone biblical literalism wherever it supplants the Lordship of the...Word of God."

— BRAD JERSAK, PHD, AUTHOR OF *A MORE CHRISTLIKE GOD*

"Keith Giles is a professional cow tipper, specializing in the sacred variety. Having toppled the sacred cow of religious nationalism in *Jesus Untangled*, he returns to the pasture in *Jesus Unbound*, where he overturns what may have become our most sacred cow of all—biblical inerrancy—along with the golden calf of biblicism that never lags far behind."

— CHUCK MCKNIGHT, BLOGGER AT HIPPIEHERETIC.COM

"In this book, Keith Giles presents us with the powerful example of his own life as he has dared to live out the prophetic insights he has discovered into the nature and mission of God's culture-challenging community. Read and gain courage to risk following his inspired and dynamic servant-leadership."

— DR SCOTT BARTCHY, PROFESSOR OF CHRISTIAN ORIGINS AND THE HISTORY OF RELIGION IN THE DEPARTMENT OF HISTORY, UCLA

OTHER BOOKS BY THE AUTHOR

- *Jesus Unexpected: Ending the End Times To Become the Second Coming*

- *Jesus Undefeated: Condemning the False Doctrine of Eternal Torment*

- *Jesus Unveiled: Forsaking Church as We Know It for Ekklesia as God Intended*

- *Jesus Unbound: Liberating the Word of God from the Bible*

- *Jesus Untangled: Crucifying Our Politics to Pledge Allegiance to the Lamb*

- *The Power of Weakness: How God Loves to Do Extraordinary Things Through Ordinary People*

- *The Gospel: For Here or to Go?*

- *The Top 10 Things Every Christian Should Know (But Probably Doesn't)*

- *Nobody Follows Jesus (So Why Should You?)*

- *[Subversive Interviews] Volume 1*

- *War Is Not Christian*

- *How To Start A Ministry To The Poor In Your Own Community*

Available online at: www.KeithGiles.com

All rights reserved. No part of this book may be used or reproduced, stored in a retrieval system, or transmitted in any form or by any means, electronic, mechanical, photocopying, recording, scanning, or otherwise, without written permission from the publisher except in the case of brief quotations embodied in critical articles and reviews. Permission for wider usage of this material can be obtained through Quoir by emailing permission@quoir.com.

Copyright © 2021 by Keith Giles.

First Edition

Cover design and layout by Rafael Polendo (polendo.net)

Unless otherwise identified, all Scripture quotations in this publication are taken from the Holy Bible, New International Version®, NIV®. Copyright ©1973, 1978, 1984, 2011 by Biblica, Inc.™ Used by permission of Zondervan. All rights reserved worldwide. www.zondervan.com The "NIV" and "New International Version" are trademarks registered in the United States Patent and Trademark Office by Biblica, Inc.™

ESV Bible® (The Holy Bible, *English Standard Version*®), copyright © 2001 by Crossway Bibles, a publishing ministry of Good News Publishers. Used by permission. All rights reserved. www.crossway.org.

ISBN 978-1-938480-77-5

This volume is printed on acid free paper and meets ANSI Z39.48 standards.

Printed in the United States of America

Published by Quoir
Oak Glen, California

www.quoir.com

JESUS
UNFORSAKEN
SUBSTITUTING DIVINE WRATH WITH UNRELENTING LOVE

KEITH GILES

THANKS TO

Matthew Distefano, Baxter Kruger, David Bentley Hart, Brad Jersak, Brian Zahnd, Bruxy Cavey, John Lynch, Dan Notti, Amy Chumbley, William Paul Young, everyone in Square 1, Square 2, Square 3 and Ground Zero. Most especially, a huge "thank you" to my wonderful wife and best friend, Wendy Giles.

DEDICATION

To my Father, Gene Giles.
There are no words for how much I love you and miss you. Thank you for everything. See you soon.

TABLE OF CONTENTS

FOREWORD

"What comes into our minds when we think about God is the most important thing about us."

— A. W. TOZER

In case you haven't heard, there is a growing debate in Christian circles. This debate is at times more of a polite discussion, and other times more of a hound howling heretic hunt. The focus of it all is on the question of why Jesus died.

From the *human* vantage point, the answer is easy—the Bible records that Jesus died because the religious leaders were threatened by the message of Jesus and appealed to the political powers for his execution. *Whenever religion and politics get in bed together, violence becomes their love child.*

From the *heavenly* vantage point, the answer is both simple and complex. Jesus said he was going to die for, among other reasons, our freedom, our healing, and to establish the New Covenant in his blood. The apostle Paul said Jesus died "for our sins" and to accomplish our "justification". But what does all this mean? How does the crucifixion of Jesus achieve what we are then invited to receive?

Since the Protestant Reformation, the dominant theory has been that when Jesus took our sin upon and into himself,

God poured out the cup of his wrath onto Christ, which in turn enabled God to forgive us all (or at least the elect). Hence, through the death of Jesus, God's justice was satisfied and his mercy expressed.

But this Atonement theory is just that—a theory. And Keith is one important voice among a growing movement of Christians who question whether it is the most biblical and the most beautiful way of understanding what Jesus accomplished on the cross. (Some Christians consider this one Atonement theory to be the gospel itself, which is a category mistake of the highest order.) I am with Keith on this journey, and I am cheering him on for writing this helpful, important contribution to the discussion.

Christians agree that God works through the crucifixion of Christ to give us eternal and abundant life. And yet, we do not agree on *how* the crucifixion of Christ accomplishes this. Thankfully, we are not reconciled to God by figuring out the metaphysics of how the cross works. We are saved by God's grace, which we simply receive by faith, not by passing an atonement theory theology exam. I'm writing this foreword during the last weeks of 2020, while we wait for a vaccine for the COVID-19 pandemic. Since I am a "high risk" person, I will be happy to trust the scientists who develop the vaccines and get one of them as soon as they are available—even though I won't have a sweet clue how it works. Thankfully, knowing how something works and trusting that it does indeed work are not the same thing.

Having said that, there is so much we can learn about who God is, about how God loves, and about who we are and can become, when we study the nature of the Atonement. We study the Atonement, not under pressure to get it right "or else", but to appreciate and celebrate the salvation we have already received. Reading this book should be joyful, encouraging, and freeing.

The Atonement (literally, At-One-Ment) is short form for God clearing away anything that stands between us and God's own heart—our fears, our failures, and our religion—so that we can be one with God. I can't think of anything more meaningful for us to spend our time investigating.

When some religious leaders couldn't understand why Jesus hung out with sinners and religious rejects, he said they should "go and learn what this means: 'I desire mercy, not sacrifice.' For I have not come to call the righteous, but sinners" (Matthew 9:12-13; see also Matthew 12:1-7). If you want to understand my subversive spirituality, says Jesus, go back into the Scriptures and focus on figuring out the meaning of this one verse—Hosea 6:6—which reads in full: "For I desire mercy, not sacrifice, and acknowledgment of God rather than burnt offerings." Jesus is giving us important instructions. If you really want to under-stand me and the God I am showing you, says Jesus, go and learn what this means. And that's what Keith Giles is helping us all do together in this excellent book.

Notice that in Hosea 6:6 God doesn't say, "I desire mercy *along with* sacrifice, and acknowledgment of God *along with* burnt offerings." No, the Bible says God wants one and *not* the other, relationship *rather than* ritual.

When the prophet Nathan confronted King David with the extent of his own sin, Nathan also introduced David to the extent of God's mercy. David was in denial about his twin evils of rape and murder, but when Nathan challenged him directly, David's eyes were opened and he immediately repented saying "I have sinned against the LORD." And what was Nathan's response to David's remorse? "The LORD has taken away your sin" (2 Samuel 12:13).

There were still real-world consequences for David because of his sin, but God's forgiveness for him was immediate, complete, and, please notice, *sans sacrifice*. Nathan never instructed David, and David never offered, to make a sacrifice, since both of them would have been aware of this sobering fact: the Bible says there is no sacrifice you can make to get forgiveness for these most serious of sins.

The Torah, the law of Moses, prescribed sacrifices primarily for *unintentional* sins (Leviticus 4-5) and some lesser *intentional* sins (Leviticus 6). But for the most severe sins like murder, adultery, and rape, the prescribed response was not sacrifice—it was the death penalty! If there was any hope for David to receive God's forgiveness, he knew it would have to be granted outside of the religious institution of animal sacrifice. For someone who committed the most serious of sins, their only hope was to cast themselves directly upon God's mercy and to invite God's forgiveness, apart from the shedding of blood. This explains why, in his great Psalm of repentance for his sin, David writes:

"Have mercy on me, O God,
  according to your unfailing love;
according to your great compassion
  blot out my transgressions.
Wash away all my iniquity
  and cleanse me from my sin.

You do not delight in sacrifice, or I would bring it;
  you do not take pleasure in burnt offerings.
My sacrifice, O God, is a broken spirit;
  a broken and contrite heart
  you, God, will not despise." (Psalm 51:1-2, 16–17)

David knew that God doesn't need blood to enable him to forgive—David's life depended on this truth! David knew what you will discover in the pages ahead: God is love, and love keeps no record of wrongs.

So, with the insight of David and the encouragement of Jesus to go and learn what it means that God has always desired mercy and not sacrifice, I commend to you this insightful and important book. Let's "go and learn" together about the heart of God, our identity as the beloved of God, and about what was really happening on the cross of Christ.

Faith, Hope, & Love,

– Bruxy Cavey
Pastor of The Meeting House and author of *The End of Religion*

PREFACE

There's a reason why this book is the sixth title in the "Jesus Un" series. Because, out of all the other topics I've covered thus far, this one is the most difficult to explain. You see, Christians already believe they understand the cross, salvation and the atonement. They've heard countless sermons about it. They're told exactly why Jesus had to die, and how they should respond to his sacrifice, and what it all means many, many times before.

The problem, as I see it, is that almost everything we've been told about the cross from the pulpit, as well as from television and radio preachers, is completely backwards from what the scriptures actually teach.

Of course, to convince people of this is nearly impossible. As long as someone believes that they know the truth, there's really no point in trying to convince them otherwise. You can't teach people who already think they know everything.

So, why am I trying to do the impossible? What is the point of

> ALMOST EVERYTHING WE'VE BEEN TOLD ABOUT THE CROSS FROM THE PULPIT, AS WELL AS FROM TELEVISION AND RADIO PREACHERS, IS COMPLETELY BACKWARDS FROM WHAT THE SCRIPTURES ACTUALLY TEACH.

writing a book about the cross and the atonement when I already know that most people won't bother to read it or take my ideas seriously?

Well, first of all, I am writing this book because I sincerely believe the Body of Christ needs to see what the atonement and the cross are really all about. Secondly, I believe that if we can at least try to see things through new eyes we might begin to experience an even deeper connection with Christ than we've ever imagined possible. Finally, I believe that the Holy Spirit has the power to open our understanding and reveal the truth to those who sincerely hunger and thirst for it.

I should also add that I believe the time is ripe for this revelation and renewal of the Christian faith. People are leaving the Evangelical church by the millions. Hundreds of thousands of people are rejecting the doctrines they were raised to believe and asking better questions about who God is and why they feel so far away from the One whose name was "Emmanuel" (God with us).

So, even though I've been accused of being a pessimist at heart, I have to admit that—at least in this case—I am becoming more and more of an optimist in terms of the potential for spiritual revolution and renewal in this day and age.

Simply put, I believe the Spirit of God is on the move like never before in my lifetime. The unease and unrest of the people in the pews is an indication that this stirring is underway. The kindling is dry. The branches are broken. The coming revolution is already being fanned into flame.

Not that I see myself, or this book, as the spark required to set things ablaze. Far from it. There are hundreds—maybe thousands—of others out there who are teaching, speaking, writing, blogging, and podcasting the radical message of this unforsaken Jesus. I'm just one voice among many other voices who all sing this song of God's amazing, inspiring and beautiful love.

Some of those voices have helped me to craft this book. For that, I am eternally grateful. We all need to recognize how much we need one another. We cannot possibly do this alone. And the great news is that we are not alone. We are one with Christ, and in the Father, and filled with the Spirit, and connected to one another in ways we haven't even begun to comprehend.

That's partly why I believe this book is so important. Because for many of you, this book may be the first time you really begin to develop a deeper understanding of what the cross is all about and what it says about who you are, and who God is.

Before we get into it much deeper, let me say this: The cross is about much more than your salvation. It's about so much more than the shedding of blood for the forgiveness of sins.

THE CROSS IS ABOUT MUCH MORE THAN YOUR SALVATION. IT'S ABOUT SO MUCH MORE THAN THE SHEDDING OF BLOOD FOR THE FORGIVENESS OF SINS.

In this book, we'll take a good hard look at the story we've all been told about the cross. We'll challenge more than one of our assumptions about why Jesus had to die and what happened that day on the old rugged cross of Calvary.

By the end of this book, if I've done what I set out to do, you will have a better understanding of the cross, the atonement, the Gospel, the Trinity, the Incarnation and salvation itself.

You may even be asked to consider some ideas that are new to you. You might feel compelled to reject certain beliefs you've held onto for a very long time.

Better yet, you may even find yourself smiling once you realize that God is better than you thought, and the Gospel is better news than you ever dared to imagine.

Thank you for being brave enough to embark on this journey with me. Now, let's take up our cross, set our eyes towards Jerusalem, and prepare to enter through the narrow gate that leads to freedom, grace and truth.

I'll be here beside you every step of the way.

THE GOSPEL UNTWISTED

"Now, before I became a Christian, I was under the impression that the first thing Christians had to believe was one particular theory as to what the point of his [Christ's] dying was. According to that theory, God wanted to punish Man for having deserted and joined the Great Rebel [Satan], but Christ volunteered to be punished instead and so God let us off. Now, I admit that even this theory does not seem quite so immoral and silly as it used to, but that is not the point that I want to make. What I came later to see is that neither this theory, nor any other, is Christianity. The central belief is that Christ's death has somehow put us right with God and given us a fresh start. Theories as to how it did this are another matter."

– C.S. LEWIS[1]

For some Christians, the Gospel and the Atonement are one and the same. In fact, when asked to explain the Gospel, many Christians today will turn to 1 Corinthians 15 and quote the Apostle Paul where he says:

> "Now, brothers and sisters, I want to remind you of the gospel I preached to you, which you received and on which you have taken your stand. By this gospel you are saved, if you hold firmly to the word I preached to you. Otherwise, you

have believed in vain. For what I received I passed on to you as of first importance: that Christ died for our sins according to the Scriptures, that he was buried, that he was raised on the third day according to the Scriptures, and that he appeared to Cephas, and then to the Twelve. After that, he appeared to more than five hundred of the brothers and sisters at the same time, most of whom are still living, though some have fallen asleep. Then he appeared to James, then to all the apostles, and last of all he appeared to me also, as to one abnormally born." (1 Corinthians 15:1–8)

Now, there are a few problems with taking this verse as our definition of the Gospel. First of all, it's not the Gospel that Jesus preached. Second, it's not the Gospel message we find in the first four books of the New Testament which are known as "The Gospels" and are individually titled "Matthew, Mark, Luke," and "John." To be honest, this paragraph from Paul's epistle to the Corinthians isn't even the Gospel that Paul himself preached. (We'll get back to that in just a minute, I promise).

So, what's going on here?

Let's start by taking a look at the Gospel that Jesus preached. To find this, we need to turn to the Gospels mentioned above. If we do, here's what we find spoken from the mouth of Jesus concerning the Gospel:

> "I must preach *the good news of the kingdom of God* to the other towns also, because that is why I was sent." (Luke 4:43, emphasis mine)

Before we get too far down the road, it might be good to point out that the "good news" Jesus is talking about is the Gospel. That's what the word "Gospel" means: "Good News," so as we read these next few verses please keep this in mind.

> "The time has come," he said. "The kingdom of God is at hand. Repent and believe *the good news!*" (Mark 1:15, emphasis mine)

"Jesus went through all the towns and villages, teaching in their synagogues, preaching *the good news of the kingdom* and healing every disease and sickness." (Matthew 9:35, emphasis mine)

"Jesus went throughout Galilee, teaching in their synagogues, preaching *the good news of the kingdom.*" (Matthew 4:23, emphasis mine)

"And *this gospel of the kingdom* will be preached in the whole world as a testimony to all nations, and then the end will come." (Matthew 24:14, emphasis mine)

In fact, Jesus spoke almost exclusively about the Kingdom of God. His parables almost always start with the phrase: "To what shall I compare the Kingdom of God? The Kingdom of God is like..." and then he would tell a parable about a man who finds a treasure in a field, or a man who seeks for precious pearls, or a woman who loses a coin, or a shepherd who seeks for his lost sheep.

Nearly everything Jesus does and says is to emphasize something about *the Gospel of the Kingdom:*

"*The kingdom of God* has come upon you." (Matthew 12:28, emphasis mine)

"For indeed, *the kingdom of God* is within you." (Luke 17:21, emphasis mine)

"After his suffering, he [Jesus] presented himself to them and gave many convincing proofs that he was alive. He appeared to them over a period of forty days and spoke *about the kingdom of God.*" (Acts 1:3, emphasis mine)

So, the Gospel message that Jesus proclaimed was all about the "Good News" of the Kingdom of God, or the Gospel of the Kingdom.

What was so good about this news of the Kingdom of God? Well, it may help to understand that the Jewish people in the

First Century were longing for a Messiah to come and establish the Kingdom of God in Jerusalem.

We might more properly say that they were looking for a Messiah who would come to "reestablish" the Kingdom of God in Jerusalem. Because what they wanted very desperately was for God to send them a warrior who would form an army and rally the people to violently overthrow the Roman Empire and set them free from this oppressive pagan state.

As you can imagine, when they started to believe that Jesus could be this Messiah it was very exciting stuff. They couldn't wait for the revolution to begin and for the regime change to take place in their lifetime. There was just one little problem: Jesus wasn't that kind of Messiah, and the Kingdom he was announcing wasn't that sort of Kingdom.

YES, JESUS WAS ABSOLUTELY LOOKING TO BRING A REGIME CHANGE TO HIS PEOPLE, BUT IT WAS ONE THAT WOULD TAKE PLACE ON THE THRONE OF THEIR HEARTS.

Yes, Jesus was absolutely looking to bring a regime change to his people, but it was one that would take place on the throne of their hearts.

The Good News of the Kingdom that Jesus proclaimed was simply this: The freedom they longed for was within their reach. The opportunity to live in the very presence of Almighty God as their victorious ruler was already possible. All they had to do was to change their way of thinking and follow this Messiah who urged them to overcome evil with good, bless the ones who cursed them, pray for those who deceitfully used them, and love the ones whom they called their worst enemies.

You can see why it didn't go over so well.

When Jesus said, "The Kingdom of God is at hand!", the people felt the rush of adrenaline and saw visions of waving banners drenched in Roman blood.

They were looking for a temporal physical kingdom. Jesus was talking about an internal eternal spiritual kingdom that would take root inside of them if they were willing to follow his path.

We have a similar problem today. When we read verses where Jesus talks about the Kingdom of God, we hear "The place we go after we die." In other words, we've been conditioned to think "Heaven" when we hear "The Kingdom of God," but that's not what Jesus was talking about either. The Gospel that Jesus preached is not about getting us into heaven after we die, it's about getting heaven into us before we die.

In other words, Jesus wants us to recognize that our accessibility into the actual living presence of the Creator of the Universe is wide open, right now. We do not need to wait until after we die to experience this awesome connection with God. It's possible to have this amazing connection with God here and now.

Now, if this is the Gospel that Jesus preached, then why doesn't it sound like what the Apostle Paul talked about in 1 Corinthians? Did Paul preach a different Gospel than Jesus?

Not at all. Just look at these verses where Paul tells us the Gospel he preached. See if you notice anything familiar about his Gospel message:

"I [Paul] have gone [among you] *preaching the kingdom of God*" (Acts 20:25, emphasis mine)

"We must go through many tribulations to enter *the kingdom of God.*" (Acts 14:22, emphasis mine)

"For *the kingdom of God* is…righteousness and peace and joy in the Holy Spirit." (Romans 14:17, emphasis mine)

"For *the kingdom of God* is not a matter of talk but of power." (1 Corinthians 4:20, emphasis mine)

"Paul entered the synagogue and spoke boldly there for three months, *arguing persuasively about the kingdom of God.*" (Acts 19:8, emphasis mine)

"He [Paul] witnessed to them from morning till evening, *explaining about the kingdom of God*, and from the Law of Moses and from the Prophets he tried to persuade them about Jesus." (Acts 28:23, emphasis mine)

"He [Paul] *proclaimed the kingdom of God* and taught about the Lord Jesus Christ—with all boldness and without hindrance!" (Acts 28:31, emphasis mine)

"Now I [Paul] know that none of you among whom *I have gone about preaching the kingdom* will ever see me again." (Acts 29:25, emphasis mine)

So, the Gospel that Paul preached and the Gospel that Jesus preached are exactly the same. They both preached the Good News of the Kingdom.

For that matter, Philip and the other Apostles also taught the Good News of the Kingdom. As we read in Acts:

"But when they believed Philip as he proclaimed *the good news of the kingdom of God* and the name of Jesus Christ, they were baptized, both men and women." (Acts 8:12, emphasis mine)

We could also look at other verses throughout the New Testament where the Apostles continued to preach and speak and teach about the very same Kingdom of God that Jesus revealed to them.[2]

Make no mistake: The Gospel that Jesus preached, and the Gospel that Paul and the other Apostles preached was one and the same—The Kingdom of God is within you!

So, what's going on in 1 Corinthians 15:1–8? Does Paul get it mixed up? Let's take another look:

"Now, brothers and sisters, I want to remind you of the gospel I preached to you, which you received and on which you have taken your stand. By this gospel you are saved, if you hold firmly to the word I preached to you. Otherwise, you have believed in vain." (1 Corinthians 15:1–2)

What we should notice here is that Paul reminds them of the Gospel he preached to them. He doesn't elaborate on the specifics of that message, but as we've already seen above, there are at least eight different verses where Paul tells us exactly what the Gospel message was: The Gospel of the Kingdom.

Now, this is where it might be a little tricky for some people. After reminding the Corinthians of the Gospel he preached to them, he then turns to another topic: the crucifixion, burial and resurrection of Christ:

"For what I received I passed on to you as of first importance: that Christ died for our sins according to the Scriptures, that he was buried, that he was raised on the third day according to the Scriptures, and that he appeared to Cephas, and then to the Twelve. After that, he appeared to more than five hundred of the brothers and sisters at the same time, most of whom are still living, though some have fallen asleep. Then he appeared to James, then to all the apostles, and last of all he appeared to me also, as to one abnormally born." (1 Corinthians 15:3–8)

If we keep in mind that Paul's Gospel message was the very same one that Jesus preached, then this isn't too difficult to manage. Paul reminds them of the Gospel of the Kingdom, and then turns to emphasize the importance of Christ's suffering, death and resurrection.

So, if Jesus defined the Gospel, and if Paul also taught the same Gospel of the Kingdom, then what are we to make of the crucifixion of Christ? What is the significance of the cross? What are we to make of Penal Substitutionary Atonement Theory?

That's what we'll be covering in our upcoming chapters.

CHAPTER 1

THEORIES OF THE ATONEMENT

"[Penal Substitutionary Atonement] is rather like a bank issuing itself credit to pay off a debt it owes itself using a currency it has minted for the occasion and certifying its value wholly on the basis of the very credit it is issuing to itself."

— DAVID BENTLEY HART

To fully understand Penal Substitutionary Atonement Theory, we should first examine the various other theories of the atonement that came before it.

Here are the main atonement theories developed over the last 1500 years:

- Recapitulation Theory [Origen, 100–165 AD]

- Ransom Theory [Irenaeus, 130–202 AD]

- Christus Victor [Similar to the Ransom Theory]

- Satisfaction Theory [Anselm, 1095 AD]

- Moral Influence Theory [Abelard, 1079–1142 AD]

- Moral Example [Faustus Socinus, 1539–1604 AD]

- Penal Substitution Theory [John Calvin, 1500s AD]

Briefly, these theories of the atonement are summarized as follows:

RECAPITULATION THEORY

In this view of the atonement, Christ is the new Adam who succeeds where Adam failed. Christ undoes the wrong that Adam did and, because of his union with humanity through the Incarnation leads all humanity into eternal life and initiates spiritual transformation.

> "Through man's disobedience the process of the evolution of the human race went wrong, and the course of its wrongness could neither be halted nor reversed by any human means. But in Jesus Christ the whole course of human evolution was perfectly carried out and realised in obedience to the purpose of God."[1]

RANSOM THEORY

As one of the earliest theories for the Atonement, this view is often held alongside the theory of Moral Influence and is concerned more with the actual death of Jesus Christ. This theory originates from the writings of both Origen and Irenaeus and teaches that Jesus died as a ransom—paid either to Satan, or to God the Father—to satisfy the debt on the souls of the human race which was inherited from Adam's original sin.

CHRISTUS VICTOR THEORY

Christus Victor emphasizes the triumph of Christ over the evil powers of the world, through which he rescues his people and establishes a new relationship between God and mankind.

"In one form or another, [the Christus Victor] view seems to have dominated the atonement theology of the early church for the first millennium (thus the label 'classic view')."[2]

In this view, *the Cross was about the victory over darkness.*

"For he [God] has rescued us from the dominion of darkness and brought us into the kingdom of the Son he loves, in whom we have redemption, the forgiveness of sins." (Colossians 1:13–14)

"When you were dead in your sins and in the uncircumcision of your flesh, God made you alive with Christ. He forgave us all our sins, having canceled the charge of our legal indebtedness, which stood against us and condemned us; he has taken it away, nailing it to the cross. *And having disarmed the powers and authorities, he made a public spectacle of them, triumphing over them by the cross.*" (Colossians 2:13–15, emphasis mine)

The Cross was also Christ's victory over Death, and the fear of Death.

"Since the children have flesh and blood, [Christ] too shared in their humanity so that by his death he might break the power of him who holds the power of death—that is, the devil—and free those who all their lives were held in slavery by their fear of death." (Hebrews 2:14–15)

SATISFACTION THEORY [ANSELM, 1095 AD]

This theory suggests that Christ redeemed humanity by offering satisfaction for humankind's disobedience. However, the word "satisfaction" does not speak of gratification but instead means "to make restitution" by making a suitable offering which satisfies the insult which mankind inflicted on God's Holy justice and honor.

MORAL INFLUENCE THEORY [ABELARD, 1079–1142 AD]

Developed specifically as an alternative to Anselm's satisfaction theory of atonement by Abelard, this theory focused on changing man's perception of God as a loving Father, not an offended tyrant. According to Abelard, "Jesus died as the demonstration of God's love,"[3] which was intended to change the hearts and minds of people and turn them back to God.

Abelard not only "rejected the idea of Jesus' death as a ransom paid to the devil," which turned the Devil into a rival god, but also objected to the idea that Jesus' death was a "debt paid to God's honor" and Anselm's emphasis on God's judgment rather than on God's love.[4]

MORAL EXAMPLE [FAUSTUS SOCINUS, 1539–1604 AD]

According to Socinus, Jesus' death offers us a perfect example of self-sacrificial dedication to God.

Although there is some close overlap between Moral Influence and Moral Example, Theologian Wayne Grudem points out their differences by noting:

> "Whereas the moral influence theory says that Christ's death teaches us how much God loves us, the example theory says that Christ's death teaches us how we should live."[5]

Author Michael Green also summarizes this view by saying:

> "The simplest and most obvious understanding of the cross is to see it as the supreme example... This is a favourite theme in the early Fathers... It can scarcely be denied that much of the second century understanding of the cross was frankly exemplarist."[6]

PENAL SUBSTITUTION THEORY [JOHN CALVIN, 1500s AD]

This view of the atonement, which originates from John Calvin during the Reformation period, says that Jesus died to satisfy God's wrath against our sins and was punished (penal) in the place of sinners (substitution) in order to satisfy the justice of God and the legal demand of God to punish sin.

In the light of Jesus' death God can now forgive the sinner because Jesus Christ has been punished in the place of the sinner; in this way meeting the retributive requirements of God's justice.

> "His [Jesus'] death was now [in the Reformation period], moreover, for the first time viewed as a vicarious punishment, inflicted by God on Him instead of on us."[7]

This theory of the Atonement contrasts with Anselm's Satisfaction Theory in that God is not satisfied with a debt of justice being paid by Jesus, but that God is satisfied with punishing Jesus in the place of mankind.[8]

CONFUSING GOSPEL WITH ATONEMENT

For many, the Gospel is expressed exclusively in terms of the Penal Substitutionary Atonement theory. This version of the Gospel is based on sacrificial atonement mechanisms derived from Old Covenant practices involving the death of an animal on an altar in a temple at the hands of a High Priest to satisfy the wrath of the Deity and result in the forgiveness of sins. Most of us are very familiar with this concept. Especially if we have spent any time in a Christian Sunday School, Bible study or Church service. We have been told this version of the Gospel so many times that we have come to accept that this mechanism *is* the Gospel itself. Especially when we hear that Jesus came to fulfill this sacrificial mandate ordained by God and that *"without the shedding of blood there is no remission of sins."* (see Hebrews 9:22)

So, what's the problem? Why is this anything to argue about? Well, as we've already seen, it really is not the Gospel that Jesus proclaimed. So, if someone convinces us that the Gospel is something other than what Jesus told us it was, that should concern us. Why replace the Gospel of the Kingdom that Jesus says he came to make known? Why reframe the Gospel as an atonement theory? What does this accomplish?

For one thing, if you manage to replace the Good News of the Kingdom with an atonement theory, you've not only silenced Jesus, you've also put everyone back under an Old Covenant sacrificial system which requires adherence to laws and observance of holiness codes. In short, you've undone the ministry of Christ and redefined His Gospel.

> **IF YOU MANAGE TO REPLACE THE GOOD NEWS OF THE KINGDOM WITH AN ATONEMENT THEORY, YOU'VE NOT ONLY SILENCED JESUS, YOU'VE ALSO PUT EVERYONE BACK UNDER AN OLD COVENANT SACRIFICIAL SYSTEM WHICH REQUIRES ADHERENCE TO LAWS AND OBSERVANCE OF HOLINESS CODES.**

But, let's not get ahead of ourselves. For a moment, let's examine this atonement theory a little more closely to see where it comes from and what it really says about God and about us.

The prevailing atonement theory in today's Christian church—at least in the Western world—is called Penal Substitutionary Atonement. It is a theory among several other theories of the atonement developed by Christian thinkers down through the centuries. Each of these atonement theories draws from previous theories and questions or corrects ideas from them to develop new theories and ideas about what was happening when Jesus died on the cross.

For nearly a millennium, the dominant view of the Christian Church was the Christus Victor Theory.[9] To this day, the Eastern Orthodox Church still embraces this view as the only one it has ever accepted regarding the atonement.

Now, let's just take a moment to consider a few things before we go any further: Christian thinkers down through the centuries have struggled to understand and to express the meaning of Christ's death on the cross. They have developed theories, offered various perspectives, submitted different ideas and worked hard to make sense of the crucifixion of Jesus. These theories of the atonement of Christ suggest that his death was a ransom, or a declaration of victory over sin and death, or an example of love and humility for us to follow, or a violent murder of an innocent man, or a final act of forgiveness for all mankind, or the means by which God reconciled the world to Himself, or a fulfillment of a sacrificial system that required blood to appease the wrath of a Holy God.

Some of these theories work to complement or verify other atonement theories. Other theories stand in stark contrast to those that have gone before and demand we choose between them. But there is one thing I think we can all agree on when it comes to these atonement theories: none of them is the Gospel that Jesus or the Apostles preached.

Now, they might be true, and they may or may not accurately explain the crucifixion of Christ upon the cross, but an atonement theory is not the Gospel, and the Gospel is not an atonement theory.

Simply put, none of these atonement theories can be called "The Gospel" because all of these theories were developed hundreds of years after the cross. Unless we maintain that the Gospel message was never preached until 400 AD, or even later, we have to admit that the Gospel was what Jesus said it was in the Gospels of the New Testament, and what the Apostles preached in the book of Acts.

We should also acknowledge that the mere existence of so many different atonement theories down through the centuries is evidence that the cross of Christ is not an easy thing to explain or to comprehend. We are still struggling in many ways to wrap our minds around the cross and to make sense of what it really means today.

We also need to admit that these atonement theories are quite often built upon metaphors that are used to frame the cross as a ransom that paid for our release from slavery, or as a sacrifice that covers our sins, or as a punishment suffered on our behalf, or perhaps as the means by which our sickness was healed. But, as with all metaphors, the more you pursue them the faster they begin to break down. For example, if the cross was a ransom payment for our release from the slavery of sin, then who got paid? What was the currency? If God paid the ransom to set us free, does that mean God owed something to Satan, or to Death, or to Lady Justice? If the cross was about removing our sins, why couldn't God just forgive us? If the cross is about healing us, couldn't God heal us without first submitting Jesus to crucifixion?

All of these theories suggest various metaphors for making sense of the cross, and to a point they all work to illuminate one aspect of what the cross may have accomplished, but in and of themselves they do not adequately explain exactly what the crucifixion was and why it happened the way it did.

As Brad Jersak points out:

> "God's saving work through Jesus is so multi-faceted that Christ and the apostles found it necessary and helpful to use a constellation of metaphors to describe its benefits. Each metaphor serves to clarify, but can also obscure. Every metaphor can extend our understanding, but can also be over-extended such that we corner ourselves into error. So our theories about the metaphors need to be held very lightly—no theory holds a monopoly on the gospel, nor should it lay claim to actually being the gospel."[10]

As we make our way through this discussion, we will try to answer some of these questions above. However, let's try to keep in mind that these theories and metaphors are not the Gospel itself. Whatever conclusions we draw from our study, our aim should be to keep sight of who Jesus is and what His Gospel message was all about. If our theory of the atonement contradicts Jesus or His Gospel, we should be willing to reconsider our conclusions and work hard to maintain our focus on Christ Himself.

IF OUR THEORY OF THE ATONEMENT CONTRADICTS JESUS OR HIS GOSPEL, WE SHOULD BE WILLING TO RECONSIDER OUR CONCLUSIONS AND WORK HARD TO MAINTAIN OUR FOCUS ON CHRIST HIMSELF.

Since the prevailing atonement theory in our day and age is the one we've called the Penal Substitutionary Atonement (or PSA) theory, our goal here is to understand what it is, where it came from, and ultimately, whether or not it is true.

UNDERSTANDING PSA THEORY

By definition, Penal Substitutionary Atonement argues that Christ, by his own sacrificial choice, was punished, or penalized, in the place of sinners (substitution) in order to satisfy the demands of justice so that God can justly forgive our sins.

As we've seen, this view was developed from ideas originated by St. Anselm around 1095 AD where he introduced his Satisfaction theory of the Atonement. But it wasn't until the rise of the Christian Reformed movement in the 1500's that the theory of Penal Substitution was fully formed under the guiding hand of John Calvin (1509–1564).

Calvin, who was trained as a lawyer, took the germ of Anselm's Satisfaction theory and redefined it to accommodate criminal law terminology. Under this new PSA theory, God is the judge, mankind has been found guilty of a crime (breaking God's Holy Law) and is deserving of an eternal punishment for this sin. Therefore, our only hope for escape from this punishment is for Jesus to become human and to suffer our penalty for us, thereby satisfying God's wrath and justice so that we can now be forgiven, healed, restored, and ultimately become recipients of God's love, mercy and grace.

Another aspect of this theory is the assumption that God is too Holy to look upon or tolerate our sinfulness, and that our sins have separated us from God. Therefore, this sinfulness needs to be dealt with and the only way to do so is to pay the penalty required for breaking God's perfect Law. This penalty is death. Although quite often the penalty is expanded to include an eternity of conscious torment in a lake of fire. Either way, the price is more than we can pay. Therefore, someone else—someone perfect and sinless and spotless—must suffer the penalty in our place in order to satisfy God's wrath and set us free from this penalty. This person, of course, is Jesus, God's only begotten Son whose death becomes a substitute for our death upon the cross.

To be fair, "the roots of the penal substitution view are discernible in the writings of John Calvin, though it was left to later expositors to systematize and emphasize it in its more robust forms."[11] But without Calvin's rephrasing of Anselm's satisfaction theory into legal terminology, the doctrine of Penal Substitution as we know it today would never have been developed.

So, while PSA theory shares some themes borrowed from other atonement theories that have come before, it remains a distinctly modern Protestant explanation of the atonement which stands in contrast to both the Eastern Orthodox and the Roman Catholic views of the atonement.

In fact, PSA theory is quite commonly considered to be the entire Gospel message itself and belief in this version of the Gospel is a required article of faith among many Evangelicals today.

In short, to deny PSA theory is to deny the Gospel (as they understand it), and therefore anyone who dares to reject this view is nothing less than a heretic, in spite of the fact that it wasn't developed until the 1500s.

Now, for those of us who have been raised to accept this analogy as the Gospel itself, PSA may seem to make a lot of sense. However, once we start to examine the theory of Penal Substitution a bit more critically, we can begin to see numerous flaws in it.

At face value, the doctrine of PSA seems to suggest that God is primarily a judge who demands justice; a God whose Holiness stands in opposition to our sinfulness; and a God whose wrath is poured out on us because we have broken His Law.

But, if this atonement theory is true, then it seems to turn verses like we find in John 3:16 upside down so that we start to believe in the exact opposite of what it teaches.

Rather than believe that "God so loved the World", we are now taught to accept the notion that God was so filled with wrath against this world of filthy sinners that He was compelled to destroy us all. Rather than believe that God's love motivated the coming of Jesus, we're asked to believe that it was in response to God's righteous anger against us. Does that sound right? Did Jesus come to save us from our sins, as the scriptures suggest, or did Jesus come to save us from His Father?

At some point we need to step back and recognize that the Gospel of the PSA theory sounds quite foreign to what we read in the actual Gospels of the New Testament.

In fact, for the first 1,000 years of Church history, nothing at all like Calvin's PSA theory was ever taught. As one scholar has noted, after Calvin's doctrine was formulated and began to spread, the way Christians thought about the crucifixion was forever changed:

"His [Jesus'] death was now [in the Reformation period], moreover, for the first time viewed as a vicarious punishment, inflicted by God on Him instead of on us."[12]

If one would embrace Calvinism's PSA version of the Gospel, then perhaps an updated version of John 3:16 would look something like this:

"For God was so filled with wrath against the world, that He sent His only begotten son to suffer the punishment that we all deserved. That if anyone would hope to escape eternal torment in the lake of fire, and would raise their hand and repeat this prayer in their hearts, they might escape this justifiable wrath of God against us all. For the son was not sent into the world to forgive us of our sins, but to suffer the righteous anger of the Father and to receive punishment for us so that God can now extend to us His perfect love and forgiveness." (John 3:16, New PSA Version)

AT SOME POINT WE NEED TO STEP BACK AND RECOGNIZE THAT THE GOSPEL OF THE PSA THEORY SOUNDS QUITE FOREIGN TO WHAT WE READ IN THE ACTUAL GOSPELS OF THE NEW TESTAMENT.

Does that make any sense to you? Hopefully, not. Perhaps you can see just how much Calvin's PSA theory twists the message of the true Gospel that Jesus proclaimed to us. Or perhaps you need a little more convincing. Nevertheless, dispensing with Calvin's theory isn't an easy thing to do. There are several elements of PSA that we need to examine and clarify before we can move on. Some of the assumptions I want to challenge in this book are:

- God requires blood sacrifice to forgive us.

- Punishment is God's response to our sinfulness.

- God's wrath is expressed in the death of Jesus.

- God is too Holy to look upon our sins.

- Jesus's death on the cross was as a substitute for us.

Let's take these one at a time.

DOES GOD REQUIRE BLOOD SACRIFICE TO FORGIVE US?

The idea that God requires blood sacrifice in order to extend forgiveness is such a core doctrine of the Christian church today that to even think of challenging this notion could threaten someone's eternal security, or at least their good standing in the local congregation.

The reflex response to this question is: Yes! God does require blood sacrifice as a prerequisite for our forgiveness. But, how do we know this? Most would automatically quote Hebrews 9:22 which says:

> "In fact, the law requires that nearly everything be cleansed with blood, and without the shedding of blood there is no forgiveness."

Case closed. There's nothing more to say, is there? Plain as day the Scripture clearly tells us: "...without the shedding of blood there is no forgiveness of sins."

But, what if there's more to this verse (and this topic of blood sacrifice) than meets the eye?

Turns out, there is. A lot more. To start with, that verse we take this idea from is part of a much larger train of thought that the author of Hebrews is in the process of developing. So, if we pull back a little and look at the entire section as a whole, we might start to notice that this passage is talking about what was required under the Old Covenant Law. In fact, the entire book of Hebrews is all about contrasting the Old Covenant Law with the "better covenant"—the New Covenant—marked by mercy, love and grace.

Therefore, in chapter 8, the author of Hebrews is in the process of contrasting "what was wrong with the first covenant" (Hebrews 8:7) with what we have now received under Christ through the New Covenant. That's why the actual quote, in context, says this:

> "In fact, *the law requires* that nearly everything be cleansed with blood, and without the shedding of blood there is no forgiveness." (Hebrews 9:22, emphasis mine)

The point the author is making is about what was necessary "under the Law" and, in context, is intended to be a critique, not an affirmation, of that Old Covenant system.

Before we go much further, we should also stop and point out that the Old Covenant isn't of one mind or voice on the topic of blood sacrifice. Moses says that God commanded His people to offer blood sacrifices:

> "[The Lord God said to Moses] Then you and the elders are to go to the king of Egypt and say to him, 'The Lord, the God of the Hebrews, has met with us. Let us take a three-day journey into the wilderness to offer sacrifices to the Lord our God.'" (Exodus 3:18)

> "'Make an altar of earth for me and sacrifice on it your burnt offerings and fellowship offerings, your sheep and goats and your cattle. Wherever I cause my name to be honored, I will come to you and bless you." (Exodus 20:24)

In fact, it's difficult to read through Exodus, Leviticus, Numbers or Deuteronomy and not come across dozens of references to sacrifices of all sorts and types being commanded by God through Moses. The same holds true for the books of Joshua, Judges, 1 and 2 Samuel, and 1 and 2 Kings, Ezra, Nehemiah, and others.

However, when we come to Isaiah and Hosea and King David in the Psalms, we uncover a very different perspective on this question of animal sacrifices.

"I gave your ancestors no commands about burnt offerings or any other kinds of sacrifices when I brought them out of Egypt. But I did command them to obey me, so that I would be their God and they would be my people. And I told them to live the way I had commanded them, so that things would go well for them." (Jeremiah 7:22-23, emphasis mine)

"What shall I bring to the Lord, the God of heaven, when I come to worship him? Shall I bring the best calves to burn as offerings to him? Will the Lord be pleased if I bring him thousands of sheep or endless streams of olive oil? Shall I offer him my first-born child to pay for my sins? No, the Lord has told us what is good. What he requires of us is this: to do what is just, to show constant love, and to live in humble fellowship with our God." (Micah 6:6-8, emphasis mine)

"The multitude of your sacrifices—what are they to me?" says the Lord. *"I have more than enough of burnt offerings, of rams and the fat of fattened animals; I have no pleasure in the blood of bulls and lambs and goats.* When you come to appear before me, *who has asked this of you,* this trampling of my courts? *Stop bringing meaningless offerings!* Your incense is detestable to me. New Moons, Sabbaths and convocations—I cannot bear your worthless assemblies. Your New Moon feasts and your appointed festivals I hate with all my being. They have become a burden to me; I am weary of bearing them." (Isaiah 1:11-14, emphasis mine)

"Listen, my people, I am speaking: Israel, I am testifying against you, I, God, your God. I am not rebuking you for your sacrifices; your burnt offerings are always before me. *I have no need for a bull from your farm or for male goats from your pens; for all forest creatures are mine already, as are the animals on a thousand hills; I know all the birds in the mountains; whatever moves in the fields is mine. If I were hungry, I would not tell you; for the world is mine, and everything in it. Do I eat the flesh of bulls or drink the blood*

of goats? Offer thanksgiving as your sacrifice to God, pay your vows to the Most High, and call on me when you are in trouble; I will deliver you, and you will honor me." (Psalm 50:7-15, emphasis mine)[13]

"You do not delight in sacrifice, or I would bring it; you do not take pleasure in burnt offerings. My sacrifice, O God, is a broken spirit; a broken and contrite heart you, God, will not despise." (Psalm 51:16-17, emphasis mine)

"For I desire mercy, not sacrifice, and acknowledgment of God rather than burnt offerings." (Hosea 6:6, emphasis mine)

"Sacrifices and grain offerings you don't want; burnt offerings and sin offerings you don't demand. (Psalm 40:6, emphasis mine)

So, if we ask Moses whether or not God requires or demands blood sacrifices we will hear an emphatic "Yes!", but if we ask Hosea, Isaiah, Jeremiah or David, we'll hear a very different response: "Not at all! God does not need, want or require sacrifices or burnt offerings from us."

In fact, if we go back to Hebrews and read a reference to the last verse quoted just above (Psalm 40:6) which provides even more context for us to consider:

> SO, IF WE ASK MOSES WHETHER OR NOT GOD REQUIRES OR DEMANDS BLOOD SACRIFICES WE WILL HEAR AN EMPHATIC "YES!", BUT IF WE ASK HOSEA, ISAIAH, JEREMIAH OR DAVID, WE'LL HEAR A VERY DIFFERENT RESPONSE: "NOT AT ALL!

"For it is impossible for the blood of bulls and goats to take away sins. Consequently, when Christ came into the world, he said, "Sacrifices and offerings you have not desired, but a body have you prepared for me; in burnt offerings and sin offerings you have taken no pleasure. Then I said, 'Behold, I have come to do your will, O God, as it is written of me in the scroll of the book.'" When he said above, "You have neither desired nor taken pleasure in sacrifices and offerings and burnt offerings and sin offerings" (these are offered according to

the law), then he added, "Behold, I have come to do your will."
He does away with the first in order to establish the second. And
by that will we have been sanctified through the offering of the
body of Jesus Christ once for all." (Hebrews 10:4-10)

So, if we break that down we'll notice a few things:

- The blood sacrifices never took away anyone's sins

- Christ affirms that God did not desire sacrifices and
  offerings

- God doesn't desire burnt or sin offerings at all

- Christ came to do God's will

- That will was *not* about blood, or sacrifices or sin offerings

- The sacrifices and sin offerings were "offered according to
  the Old Covenant law"

- That Old Covenant law was a defective covenant (See
  Hebrews 8:7;13)

- Christ did away with the first covenant (the Old Covenant)
  in order to establish the "better [new] covenant"

- When Christ submitted to the will of God, it was to fulfill
  the Law and the Prophets [thereby making them obsolete
  (Hebrews 8:13)

If we can follow this train of thought, then the next part
should be easier to understand.

Because we understand that God never wanted blood sacrifices, and that those sacrifices never took way anyone's sins, we
can see that God's will was about something else—something
not related to offering any sacrifices for sin—but about fulfilling

the Old Covenant to establish the New Covenant. (We'll talk more about this very soon.)

So, our sanctification is established "through the offering of the body of Jesus Christ once for all" (as it says in Hebrews 10:10 above), but we must be very careful not to slip back into blood sacrifice mode here. The idea of the offering of the body of Jesus Christ is not affirming the very notion we just spent so much time unpacking in the verses above this.

The "offering of the body of Jesus" is not a picture of Jesus being sacrificed to appease God's wrath or fulfill God's justice. Instead, it is a picture of Christ's obedience to the will of God—which we remember is *not* about sacrifice.

As Hosea phrased it: God desires mercy, not sacrifice. Jesus echoes this when he reminds the Pharisees: "Go and learn what this means: 'I desire mercy, not sacrifice." (Matthew 9:13)

Mercy here is expressed in the way we love one another. What God requires of us is that we "Do justice, love mercy and walk humbly with our God" (Micah 6:8). God does not want our sacrifice. God wants us to love one another as we have been loved.

So, the "offering of the body of Jesus" is best described in Philippians 2 where the Apostle Paul shows us a clear picture of just how much Jesus sacrificed in the Incarnation:

> "[consider] Christ Jesus, who, though he was in the form of God, did not count equality with God a thing to be grasped, but emptied himself, by taking the form of a servant, being born in the likeness of men. And being found in human form, he humbled himself by becoming obedient to the point of death, even death on a cross." (Philippians 2:5-8)

Jesus laid down his life for us by letting go of his glorified status to "empty himself" and by "taking the form of a servant" he humbled himself even "to the point of death...on a cross." So, his "sacrifice" for us was in the manner in which he emptied himself and offered his entire life to us as one who "did not come to be served, but to serve" all humanity. This was the "offering of the body of Jesus" which is in view in Hebrews 10:10.

We also must understand that what is being communicated in Philippians 2 above is that Christ Jesus let go of immortality to become enfleshed in mortality. The "offering of the body of Jesus" is only possible because Jesus took on flesh, and that meant becoming mortal. Therefore, death was always inevitable in the equation of the incarnation. Once Jesus became human, his death was guaranteed. One way or the other, Jesus was going to die. The question for us then becomes: Was crucifixion the only acceptable way for Jesus to die? Or would his death have the same salvific significance either way? We'll examine that question in just a moment. For now, let's finish the question about blood sacrifice as a requirement for our forgiveness.

> THE "OFFERING OF THE BODY OF JESUS" IS ONLY POSSIBLE BECAUSE JESUS TOOK ON FLESH, AND THAT MEANT BECOMING MORTAL. THEREFORE, DEATH WAS ALWAYS INEVITABLE IN THE EQUATION OF THE INCARNATION.

As we've seen so far, the Old Testament scriptures are not in agreement when it comes to the question of blood sacrifices for the forgiveness of sins. Moses says yes. Isaiah, Jeremiah, Hosea and David say no. Jesus seems to agree with them, especially when he quotes Hosea directly, affirming that God desires mercy, not sacrifice. And here in the book of Hebrews it would seem that this denial of the requirement for blood sacrifice is also affirmed quite emphatically.

But there's even more to consider before we make up our minds completely.

For example, there are seven examples from the Old Testament where God says that people's sins are forgiven without the shedding of blood. In these passages below, forgiveness is granted on the basis of:

- Application of oil (Leviticus 14:29)

- Burning flour (Leviticus 5:11–13)

- Burning incense (Numbers 16:41–50)

- Payment of money (Exodus 30:11–16)

- Gifts of jewelry (Numbers 31:48–54)

- The release of a live animal (a scapegoat) into the wilderness (Leviticus 16:10)

- Simple appeals to God through prayers (Exodus 32:30; Psalm 32; 51; 103)

We also have a quite famous example in 2 Chronicles where forgiveness was extended to the entire Nation of Israel based solely on prayer and repentance:

> "If my people who are called by my name humble themselves, pray, seek my face, and turn from their wicked ways, then I will hear from heaven, and will forgive their sin and heal their land." (2 Chronicles 7:14)

There is no mention of blood sacrifice being offered in any of these passages above. Forgiveness is granted because God is good and responds to our failures with mercy.

As the Psalmist proclaims:

> "[For God] does not treat us as our sins deserve or repay us according to our iniquities. For as high as the heavens are above the earth, so great is his love for those who fear him; as far as the east is from the west, so far has he removed our transgressions from us." (Ps. 103:10–12)

So, sin offerings are not always required, and even where sacrifices are mentioned there are often exceptions made, as when
the poor are allowed to offer a grain offering if they cannot afford
to bring an animal to sacrifice—and forgiveness is still granted,
without any bloodshed.(See Leviticus 5:11–13)

Therefore, it would seem that our default understanding of
what is required for the forgiveness of sins is seriously in question. God most certainly *does* offer the forgiveness of sins *without*
the shedding of blood.

This should not surprise us. If we take a moment to think
about it, the sort of God who demands blood sacrifice in order
to forgive our sins looks a lot more like Baal or Molech than the
Abba Father revealed to us by Jesus.

So, where did this idea come from? How did we ever come
to believe that God—the true God of the Scriptures—was even
remotely like those pagan deities who required blood sacrifices
to be appeased?

The answer is found by going all the way back to the very
beginning when Abraham—the Father of the Jewish faith—first
heard the voice of God. Prior to this it's very likely that Abraham
worshipped other gods. He was in his nineties by this time, so
he would've had a lifetime of idol worship experience to color
his ideas about this new God who had suddenly spoken to him.

Remember, this is was before Moses, before the Law, before
the Tabernacle or the Temple. God had not fully revealed
Himself in this way to anyone yet. So, Abraham didn't have the
benefit of a Torah, or a Bible, or even a single one of the Ten
Commandments to guide him. All he knew was there was a God
who had spoken to him and promised to bless him and his seed
to come.

This is most likely why God tested Abraham regarding the
sacrifice of his own son. Such a thing would've been seen as

normal to someone in Abraham's day. The other gods that he would've known about would often require the sacrifice of a child to prove one's loyalty and obedience. Why should this God be any different?

But that was the point. This God was different. This God wanted Abraham to know that He was not like all those other gods who required human sacrifice.

> **UNDER THIS PSA THEORY, THE FATHER OF JESUS IS ONE WHO WILL NOT SETTLE FOR ANYTHING LESS THAN A VIRGIN, PURE, SPOTLESS HUMAN SACRIFICE—EVEN HIS OWN SON—IN ORDER TO APPEASE HIS WRATH.**

Yet, somehow, Calvin's doctrines have convinced Christians today that God does require a human blood sacrifice, and that without the shedding of blood He cannot—and does not—forgive sins. Under this PSA theory, the Father of Jesus is one who will not settle for anything less than a virgin, pure, spotless human sacrifice—even His own son—in order to appease His wrath.

You might take some offense at the way I phrased that, but if we compare the pagan volcano gods of the primitive world to the God described by Calvin and his PSA theory of the atonement, we might see that this comparison is not far off.

PAGAN GOD	CALVIN'S GOD
Is angry	Full of wrath
Requires sacrifice	Demands the shedding of blood
Must be human	Humans deserve death for sins
Must be a virgin	Jesus was sinless [and a virgin]
Is appeased after the sacrifice	The death of Jesus turns away wrath

This is another reason why the Penal Substitutionary Atonement theory is so offensive: It portrays God as one who looks more like Molech or Zeus than the Abba Father God revealed through Christ.

This is also why it's dangerous to call this "The Gospel" because it is as far from the "Good News" message that Jesus proclaimed as possible.

Not only is this atonement theory a distortion of the character of God, it's also something totally foreign to the doctrines of the early Christian church. As one Church Historian (H.N. Oxenham) points out so emphatically:

> "...we may pause to sum up briefly the main points of teaching on Christ's work of redemption to be gathered from the patristic literature of the first three centuries as a whole. And first, as to what it does not contain. There is no trace, as we have seen, of the notions of vicarious satisfaction, in the sense of our sins being imputed to Christ and His obedience imputed to us, which some of the Reformers made the very essence of Christianity; or, again, of the kindred notion that God was angry with His Son for our sakes, and inflicted on Him the punishment due to us ; nor is Isaiah's prophecy interpreted in this sense, as afterwards by Luther; on the contrary, there is much which expressly negates this line of thought. There is no mention of the justice of God, in the forensic sense of the word; the Incarnation is invariably exclusively ascribed to His love; the term satisfaction does not occur in this connection at all, and where Christ is said to suffer for us, huper (not anti) is the word always used. It is not the payment of a debt, as in St. Anselm's Cur Deus Homo, but the restoration of our fallen nature, that is prominent in the minds of these writers, as the main object of the Incarnation. They always speak, with Scripture, of our being reconciled to God, not of God being reconciled to us."[14]

These are excellent points that we would do well to consider. First, that the early Christians did not speak of our sins being laid upon Christ, or of His obedience being credited to us, as

Calvin suggests. Secondly, that the early Church never spoke of God as one who poured out His wrath upon Christ; as if it was Jesus who took the bullet meant for us and suffered the punishment we deserved.

Please take some time to meditate on these facts. The Christian Church never thought this way for over 1,500 years. It wasn't until Calvin came along and imported his own ideas about God as a Judge demanding justice in the Cosmic Courtroom that these concepts were first introduced.

Prior to this, the Christian community saw God as a Father who loved us and sent His Son as a messenger of reconciliation who came not to change God's mind about us, but to change our minds about God.

Now, let's take a look at the next tenet of Penal Substitution Atonement theory.

IS PUNISHMENT GOD'S RESPONSE TO SIN?

Much like the idea above, many of us have an instinctive response to this question that comes from years of sitting through sermons and Bible studies where the only answer anyone could ever give to this would be "Yes!"

However, once we start to dig a little deeper, we might want to reconsider our kneejerk response.

For example, Jesus told us that he only did what he saw the Father doing, (John 5:19). So, if we look at Jesus we should be able to get a pretty good idea what God would do in a similar situation. (See John 14)

If we see Jesus showing compassion to the poor, for example, we can safely conclude that God must also have compassion on the poor, because Jesus is the clearest picture anyone could have of who God is and what God is like.

As the author of Hebrews affirms:

"He [Jesus] is the radiance of the glory of God and the exact imprint of his nature.." (Hebrews 1:3)

So, when it comes to sin, Jesus has a very curious response. Each and every time Jesus encounters a sinner he does something amazing: He forgives them!

Even if that person does not ask Jesus for forgiveness, Jesus still forgives that person automatically. It's true. In fact, I invite you to read through the Gospels and underline all the times Jesus tells someone "Your sins are forgiven." Then, take note of how quickly Jesus says this. If you do this, you'll notice that Jesus usually forgives that person before they've even opened their mouth to ask him anything at all.

Here's the evidence we find when we look at Jesus: God responds to our sinfulness with forgiveness. Because Jesus forgives everyone, all the time, therefore, God also forgives everyone, all the time.

How does Jesus respond to our sins? He forgives. Completely. Automatically. One hundred percent.

Jesus never waited for anyone to repent. Jesus never asked anyone to confess their sins first. Jesus never did anything but forgive everyone he met; every single time.

Jesus even forgave those unbelieving pagan Roman soldiers who were in the very process of murdering him by nailing him to the cross. If Jesus could forgive people like this so freely, who could ever be exempt?

What's more, those Roman soldiers never asked for forgiveness. They didn't even believe that Jesus

HERE'S THE EVIDENCE WE FIND WHEN WE LOOK AT JESUS: GOD RESPONDS TO OUR SINFULNESS WITH FORGIVENESS. BECAUSE JESUS FORGIVES EVERYONE, ALL THE TIME, THEREFORE, GOD ALSO FORGIVES EVERYONE, ALL THE TIME.

was the Messiah or the Son of God. Yet, Jesus forgives them anyway.

As Paul the Apostle affirms:

> "…that God was in Christ reconciling the world to himself, not counting people's sins against them." (2 Corinthians 5:19)

So, God's primary response to our sins is forgiveness, not punishment. As the great Karl Barth once said:

> "…we must not make this [the concept of punishment] a main concept as in some of the older presentations of the doctrine of the atonement (especially those which follow Anselm of Canterbury), within the sense that by His [Christ's] suffering our punishment we are spared from suffering it ourselves, or that in so doing He "satisfied" or offered satisfaction to the wrath of God. The latter thought is quite foreign to the New Testament."[15]

And C.S. Lewis also weighed in on Penal Substitutionary Atonement theory in *Mere Christianity* saying:

> "[PSA theory is] the one about our being let off because Christ had volunteered to bear a punishment instead of us. Now on the face of it that is a very silly theory. If God was prepared to let us off, why on earth did He not do so? And what possible point could there be in punishing an innocent person? None at all that I can see, if you are thinking of punishment in the police-court sense. On the the other hand, if you think of a debt, there is plenty of point in a person who has some assets paying it on behalf of someone who has not."[16]

But, what about those verses in the Bible that *do* mention punishment? What about the scriptures that talk about the wages of our sins being death? What about the "wrath of God" that comes whenever people disobey His commands?

Great questions. Let's answer those next.

WHAT ABOUT THE WRATH OF GOD?

Thanks to the doctrine handed down to us from John Calvin in the 1500s, most of us cannot imagine God any other way than as a Judge who sits in the cosmic courtroom of Heaven passing judgement upon all who break His Holy Law.

God's wrath is so ingrained in us that we can hardly think of God apart from it. Many Christian pastors and Bible Teachers have even gone so far as to assure us that God is not only a God of love, but also, and perhaps even more so, a God of wrath.

For example:

"A study of the concordance will show that there are more references in Scripture to the anger, fury, and wrath of God, than there are to His love and tenderness. Because God is holy, He hates all sin; And because He hates all sin, His anger burns against the sinner." (A.W. Pink, *The Attributes of God*, chapter 16.)

"The cliché, God hates the sin but love the sinner, is false on the face of it and should be abandoned. Fourteen times in the first fifty Psalms alone, we are told that God hates the sinner, His wrath is on the liar, and so forth. In the Bible, the wrath of God rests both on the sin and on the sinner." (D.A. Carson, *The Difficult Doctrine of the Love of God*, Crossway Books, 2000, pg.70.)

"God's wrath arises from His intense, settled hatred of all sin and is the tangible expression of His inflexible determination to punish it. We might say God's wrath is His justice in action, rendering to everyone his just due, which, because of our sin, is always judgment." (Jerry Bridges, *The Gospel For Real Life*, Navpress, 2002, pg. 52.)

"As God's mercies are new every morning toward His people, so His anger is new every morning against the wicked." (Matthew Henry)

What is our response to all of this? Is it true that God is a God of wrath?

IS GOD'S WRATH EXPRESSED IN THE DEATH OF JESUS?

The Wrath of God is a key pillar in Calvin's PSA Theory. God's wrath is His righteous anger against not just "sin" itself, but against "sinners", too.

Make no mistake, according to those who embrace PSA, God does not "hate the sin and love the sinner." He hates them both.

> "The moment you take your first step through the gates of hell, the only thing you will hear is all of creation standing to its feet and applauding and praising God because God has rid the earth of you. That's how not good you are." (Paul Washer)

> "God does not punish innocent children for the sins of guilty parents. There are no innocent children" (John Piper)

> "Some of you, God hates you. Some of you, God is sick of you. God is frustrated with you. God is wearied by you. God has suffered long enough with you. He doesn't think you're cute. He doesn't think it's funny." (Mark Driscoll)

To those who believe in PSA theory, the wrath of God has become synonymous with God's character. God *is* a wrathful God. Not merely a God of Love, but equally so a God whose wrath defines Him and drives everything He does.

Of course, there are no verses that say "God *is* wrath", but there are verses that affirm "God is Love", for example:

> "Whoever does not love does not know God, because God is love." (1 John 4:8)

Other verses promise us that "God's anger [wrath] is for a moment, but His favor [love] endures forever." (See Psalm 30:5; 136:1)

What many of us seem to have missed is the subversive way that the scriptures often speak about the Wrath of God.

So, if we ever read any verses that talk about the wrath of God, or the judgment of God, or anything else, we need to always filter that through the understanding that God is love. That means the wrath of God is always understood through the realization that God is love. Another way to phrase it might be to say: "The wrath of the God who is love," or "The wrath of a loving God."

My friend Steve Kline shared his thoughts on this as he was inspired by something he noticed in Psalm 18:25-27 which says:

> "With the merciful you show yourself merciful; with the blameless you show yourself blameless; with the purified you show yourself pure; and with the crooked you make yourself seem tortuous." (Psalm 18:25–27)

Here's what Steve took from this passage:

> "The conception among most Christians is that God is angry with us and that if we don't repent then He will pour out His wrath on us...Yes, we have sinned horribly against God. We denied him...For that, we must repent if we want to enter the kingdom of God, the kingdom of heaven, eternal life.
>
> "...But, for those that don't repent, is it God's wrath that will be poured out on them? Or, is it the lies and the violence of the unrepentant themselves that will come back on their own head? Throughout the Bible, we see that the pit the wicked dug they themselves fall into. Or, the snare that evil people set they get caught in themselves. And, in the depictions of Satan (for example, Goliath and Haman), he is almost always killed with his own weapon."
>
> "The repentant have become merciful, blameless, and purified. And, to the repentant God shows Himself as such. But, to the unrepentant, the crooked (in Psalm 18), God makes Himself seem tortuous. It seems to them like God is vengeful, spiteful, and vindictive, pouring His wrath out on them. However, in

reality, it is their own lies and violence that are coming back on their own heads."[17]

I believe this is a key insight—from the Scriptures—that we need to take seriously. The wrath of God is quite often something experienced as the fruit of one's own actions rather than as the direct action of God against the unrighteous. Or perhaps even more along the lines of the sowing and reaping principle outlined several times throughout scripture.

So, our perception of God as a God of Wrath might say more about us than about God. If we are wrathful, then we may experience God as being wrathful. But, if we are loving and merciful, God may show Himself to us as love and mercy.

THE WRATH

As David Bentley Hart clarifies, the phrase "Wrath of God" in our English Bibles may not exactly belong there:

"In the Rabbinic tradition, the concept of "ire" or "wrath" is simply a metaphor for God's Holiness within the experience of correction. It is certainly not an emotional attribute of God. God is not one who has a mutable psychological personality. Augustine himself points out that God doesn't get angry. He never suggests that. Nonetheless, we must be careful because the term 'wrath of God' is not alien to the New Testament, but it shows up in our translations more often than it should. *Paul will sometimes speak of "The Wrath" and some translators will render that "The Wrath of God", when it's clear that he means "The Wrath of the Law"*, as if the wrath has a somewhat cosmic power set in motion by the Law, probably under angelic governance. *So, "the wrath of God" is more plentifully present in the [English] translations than it is in the original Greek. It is the wrath of the Law that only has the power to condemn as set off against the mercy of God [in Christ].*" (emphasis mine)[18]

This point is quite significant if you understand to what lengths Paul often goes to contrast the Old Covenant (the Law) with the New Covenant (Life in Christ).

So, it's very likely that when we read "the wrath of God", especially in the New Testament, we should probably recognize that Paul may be referring to the Law of Sin and Death as it pales in comparison to the New Covenant promise of life, grace and mercy through Jesus Christ.

For example, Paul speaks in 2 Corinthians 3:7 of "the ministry that brought death, which was engraved on letters of stone" which clearly refers to the 10 Commandments and the Law of Moses. Then he turns to contrast this with the ministry of Christ:

> "If the ministry that condemns men [the Old Covenant] is glorious, how much more glorious is the ministry that brings righteousness! [the New Covenant] For what was glorious [the Old] has no glory now in comparison with the surpassing glory. And if what was fading away [the Old] came with glory, how much greater is the glory of that which lasts! [the New]" (2 Corinthians 3:7–11)

The point here seems to be more about how the Law carries condemnation. "The wrath" here is not from God. It seems that it is only referenced in terms of the fruit of sin and the death it produces in us apart from Christ.[19]

THE WRATH OF THE BABY LAMB

One of my favorite examples of how the New Testament subverts this idea of the wrath of God is when we are told about the "Wrath of the Lamb" in Revelation. As my friend Richard Murray notes:

> "Jesus is the Lamb of God. So He, by extension, is the wrath of God personified [in Revelation 6:16]. But here is the thing: Lambs have no wrath. So, the term is an oxymoron. It's an

image clash where wrath itself is deconstructed by the jarring contradiction of two incompatible terms. This then allows divine wrath to be conceptually recast as the restorative and curative energies of God.

"So let's look at both God's birth statement and death statement regarding Jesus as the revelation of 'the wrath of God.'

"Here is the divine wrath statement given by angelic pronouncement at His birth: 'Peace on earth, goodwill to man.' (Luke 2:14)

"Hmmm. And here is His bookend statement on the issue of wrath at His death: 'Forgive them Father, for they know not what they do.' (Luke 23:34)

"Hmmm. The 'wrath of the Lamb' is now revealed: Peace, goodwill, and forgiveness toward all men!"

This same oxymoron is further exemplified in David Bentley Hart's translation of the New Testament where he notes that the "Lamb" in Revelation 5:6 is more accurately rendered as "the suckling lamb", which is the equivalent of a kitten or a newborn puppy.

As Hart puts it:

"Not arnos or arnen—a 'lamb'—but an arnion—literally, a 'little lamb' or 'lambkin', a term most properly applied to a lamb that is still nursing."

So, this image of Christ as the "suckling lamb" or "newborn lambkin" further challenges the notion that the "wrath of the Lamb" is anything other than an intentionally jarring mashup of clashing ideas that should lead us to rethink our notions of the Wrath of God.

Are you terrified at the notion of enraging a kitten? Do you tremble at the thought of falling under the fearsome wrath of a puppy? Of course not. Yet, this is exactly why John uses such unexpected language in Revelation; to emphasize the ridiculousness of the notion that anyone should ever fear the Wrath of the Baby Lamb. Lambs have no wrath. This is the very point he wants us to understand.[20]

Simply put: God is love. God is not wrath. God is not judgment. God is exactly like Jesus who freely forgives us and heals us. His love endures forever. And it's the kindness of God that leads us all to repentance.

If wrath and vengeance were truly attributes of God's character and reflections of His Divine Nature, then we might expect to see these listed alongside the other Fruits of the Spirit found in the Scriptures.

ARE YOU TERRIFIED AT THE NOTION OF ENRAGING A KITTEN? DO YOU TREMBLE AT THE THOUGHT OF FALLING UNDER THE FEARSOME WRATH OF A PUPPY? OF COURSE NOT.

After all, the Fruit of the Spirit is simply a reflection of the nature and character of God imparted to us by the Holy Spirit as we abide in Christ. These attributes— love, joy, peace, patience, kindness, gentleness and self-control— are Divine attributes.

We bear these fruits because we are being transformed by the Spirit of God into people who reflect the image and nature of God as revealed in Christ.

Wrath is not an attribute of God's nature. Vengeance is not a reflection of God's heart. What we see in the Suckling Lamb is the true face of God who is not wrathful, but loving and merciful.[21]

PUNISHMENT REEXAMINED

When the scriptures speak about punishment for our sins, it's not always so clear what is meant if we rely solely upon our modern English translations to guide us. Quite often the translators are trying a little too hard to push the scriptures into alignment with certain doctrines that the publishers want to promote.

There are numerous examples of these kinds of translation errors and biases in my previous book, *Jesus Unbound: Liberating the Word of God from the Bible*, but our concern here is specifically how translators may have worded those verses that deal with punishment and sin in relation to Christ and His crucifixion.

The early Patristic Church Fathers who lived in the golden season of Church history prior to the rise of Constantine took a very different view of the Atonement than modern PSA-influenced Christians do today.

Many of our English Bibles tend to include the word "Propitiation" in Romans 3:23–25 as we see here in the New American Standard translation:

> "…For all have sinned and fall short of the glory of God, being justified as a gift by His grace through the redemption which is in Christ Jesus; whom God displayed publicly as a *propitiation* in His blood through faith." (emphasis mine)

This term (Propitiation) suggests the need for restitution or appeasement. But as author Brad Jersak points out, there is a better, and more accurate way, of understanding those passages:

> "Propitiation" is how some translators have rendered the Greek word "Hilasterion", but it is very difficult word to translate into English because when we do we seem to keep trying to import ideas of appeasing wrath, which is a rather pagan way of viewing God and sacrifice. So, this is why we sometimes translate "Hilasterion" as "Propitiation" and that's a very odd choice of words because it's about wrath-appeasement…Did God's wrath need appeasement? Is that what we see in the Parable of the Prodigal Son?…some translators translate Hilasterion as "Expiation" which is more about the removal of our sin or our guilt, or perhaps making amends for things and setting things right again. But that doesn't quite say it either.

"In the Septuagint—the Greek translation of the Old Testament—we find this word "Hilasterion" too and it always describes it in this way; as a Mercy Seat like we find on the Ark of the Covenant. So, the cross becomes the Mercy Seat where God and humanity are reconciled. How? As God forgives—rather than punishing—our sins. When we pour out our wrath on God's Son, instead of taking vengeance on us, He hears His Son's prayer "Father, forgive them for they know not what they do.""[22]

So, if we can agree that God is not like the volcano god who demands appeasement or sacrifice in order to satisfy His wrath and extend forgiveness to us, then perhaps we can begin to see how the term *"Hilasterion"* is better understood as being an extension of God's love and mercy to everyone.

Taking another look at that passage in Romans above, we may also begin to see what the verse is really saying to us about how a loving Father responds to our sins if we read the entire passage in context, paying close attention to the very end of that verse:

"...For all have sinned and fall short of the glory of God, being justified as a gift by His grace through the redemption which is in Christ Jesus; whom God displayed publicly *as an atonement* in His blood through faith. *This was to demonstrate His righteousness, because in the forbearance of God He passed over the sins previously committed...*" (Romans 3:23–25, emphasis mine)

Again, the entire point here is that God, through Christ, offered an atonement leading to reconciliation in order to demonstrate His righteousness and to forgive our sins once and for all. This is not a picture of an angry, wrathful God who demands restitution or appeasement before anyone can be forgiven. Far from it! It is a picture of a loving God who goes out of His way to extend mercy to us through Christ so that we can be reconciled to God and be set free from our sins.

There is no wrath here. Nor is there any wrath in God's heart towards His children, only love, mercy, forgiveness and reconciliation.

> "Herein is love: not that we loved God, but rather that God loved us and sent his Son as an atonement for our sins." (1 John 4:10)

The atonement we see in the cross of Christ is not about wrath. It's about love.

To put a final point on the issue, let's listen to what French Jesuit theologian and biblical scholar Stanislas Lyonnet has to say about the use of the term *Hilasterion* in 1 John:

> "When St. John in two different places alludes first to the heavenly intercession of Christ before the Father (1 John 2.2), and then to the work accomplished here below by His death and resurrection (1 Jn 4.10), he declares that [Christ] is or that the Father has made Him a hilasmos for our sins.' This term certainly carries the same meaning which it always has in O.T. Greek (Vulgate Ps 130.4) and which the Latin word propitiatio also always conveys in the liturgy: through Christ and in Christ, the Father achieves the plan of His eternal love (1 Jn 4.8) in 'showing Himself propitious,' that is in 'pardoning' men, by an efficacious pardon which really destroys sins, which 'purifies' man and communicates to him God's own life (1 Jn 4.9)."[23]

As we can see, the entire thing is entirely based on the notion of a Father who "loved us and sent his Son as atonement for our sins." (1 John 4:10)

We'll continue to unpack this notion of the "Wrath of God" in more detail very soon. For now, let's look at the nature of God's response to our sin.

RETRIBUTION OR RESTORATION?

There are a few passages that deal with how God punishes our sins, but what we see if we look closely is that God's correction is always about restoration and never about exacting retribution.

Here are a few examples:

"For [God] will be like a refiner's fire or a launderer's soap. He will sit as a refiner and purifier of silver." (Malachi 3:2–3)

The fire and the soap are both about purification, not punishment. The refiner's fire is what purifies the gold and silver, removing the impurities to reveal the pure value of the metal, and launderer's soap is about cleansing us to restore us to our original goodness.

"For no one can lay any foundation other than the one already laid, which is Jesus Christ. If anyone builds on this foundation using gold, silver, costly stones, wood, hay or straw, their work will be shown for what it is, because the Day will bring it to light. It will be revealed with fire, and the fire will test the quality of each person's work. If what has been built survives, the builder will receive a reward. If it is burned up, the builder will suffer loss but yet will be saved—even though only as one escaping through the flames." (1 Corinthians 3:11–15)

Here, Paul affirms that the purpose and nature of God's fire judgment is all about revealing the righteousness of Christ in us. However, even if one has no righteousness of Christ in himself at all—if everything is consumed in the fire because there is nothing of Christ to be revealed—salvation will still be the result of that process "as one escaping through the flames." In other words, the person will not be consumed or burned by the fire of God's judgment. Salvation is the result, no matter what condition the person was in before they entered that fire.

As Jesus affirms, "Everyone will be salted with fire" (Mark 9:49), so this fire of judgement is something everyone will experience, but the purpose of that fire—once again—is to purify, restore and transform us into the image of Christ.

I believe our best picture of how God responds to our sinfulness is outlined for us in Hebrews 12:5–12:

> "And have you forgotten the exhortation that addresses you as sons? "My son, do not regard lightly *the discipline of the Lord,* nor be weary when reproved by him. For *the Lord disciplines the one he loves, and chastises every son whom he receives."* It is for discipline that you have to endure. *God is treating you as sons. For what son is there whom his father does not discipline?* If you are left without discipline, in which all have participated, then you are illegitimate children and not sons. Besides this, we have had earthly fathers who disciplined us and we respected them. Shall we not much more be subject to the Father of spirits and live? For they disciplined us for a short time as it seemed best to them, but *he disciplines us for our good, that we may share his holiness. For the moment all discipline seems painful rather than pleasant, but later it yields the peaceful fruit of righteousness to those who have been trained by it."* (emphasis mine)

Here, we see a beautiful explanation of how God approaches discipline and correction with an end result in mind—"that we may share His holiness" and enjoy "the peaceful fruit of righteousness."

In other words, God's discipline and correction is always for our good; it is always intended to restore us and renew us into the image of Christ.

Now, let's look at the next pillar of Calvin's Penal Substitutionary Atonement Theory.

IS GOD TOO HOLY TO LOOK UPON OUR SINS?

The idea that God's Holiness separates us from Himself is another popular teaching in pulpits where Calvin's theology has taken root. In fact, this notion is so widely accepted in Christianity today that this bedrock assumption is what forms the basis for many other doctrines and teachings.

The way many Christians evangelize begins with this idea. We tell unbelievers that their sinfulness separates them from God because He is Holy and, therefore, they cannot survive in His presence, and conversely that God cannot tolerate our offensive presence due to our sinfulness.

This same notion of God's Holiness is what drives our concepts of Eternal Torment for those who deny Christ. God has no choice but to toss them into the Lake of Fire prepared for the Devil and his angles because their sinfulness and His perfect Holiness can never coexist together.

But is this what the Bible says about God's Holiness? Do the scriptures affirm this notion that our sins prevent us from being in God's presence? Is God really too Holy to look upon our sins?

> IN OTHER WORDS, GOD'S DISCIPLINE AND CORRECTION IS ALWAYS FOR OUR GOOD; IT IS ALWAYS INTENDED TO RESTORE US AND RENEW US INTO THE IMAGE OF CHRIST.

If we start to search for verses that affirm this idea, we suddenly find ourselves floundering for the evidence. Instead, what we see is that all throughout the Bible, God *does* indeed look at mankind.

For example, just read these verses about how much God looks at people in their sins:

> "For the eyes of the Lord run to and fro throughout the whole earth, to give strong support to those whose heart is blameless toward him." (2 Chronicles 16:9)

> "Does not [God] see my ways and number all my steps?" (Job 31:4)

> "For my eyes are on all their ways. They are not hidden from me, nor is their iniquity concealed from my eyes." (Jeremiah 16:17)

"These...are the eyes of the Lord, which range through the whole earth." (Zechariah 4:10)

"And there is no creature hidden from His sight, but all things are open and laid bare to the eyes of Him with whom we have to do." (Hebrews 4:13)

So much for the notion that God is too Holy to look upon our sins. But, this shouldn't really surprise us. Just imagine what would happen if God wasn't able to look at sin? That would mean that God could never see anything on the Earth at all. God would, in effect, become blinded by our sinfulness, and His own Holiness.

It turns out that this doctrine that God is too holy to look upon sin is based on one single verse of scripture in the Old Testament that says:

"Your eyes are too pure to look on evil; you cannot tolerate wrongdoing." (Habbukuk 1:13)

But if we keep reading that same chapter what we notice is that Habbukuk wraps up that statement by essentially asking: *"So, why do you?"*

In other words, the question is asked assumptively, but then the question itself is cast into doubt as the prophet observes that God does indeed look on evil after all.

Another verse that is often used to support this idea that God is too holy to look upon our sins is found in Isaiah where we read:

"But your iniquities have separated you from your God; your sins have hidden his face from you, so that he will not hear." (Isaiah 59:2)

Once again, if we simply keep reading we will come across this verse that says:

"The Lord looked and was displeased that there was no justice. He saw that there was no one, he was appalled that there was no one to intervene; so his own arm achieved salvation for him, and his own righteousness sustained him." (v. 16)

"As for me, this is my covenant with them," says the Lord. "My Spirit, who is on you, will not depart from you..." (v. 21)

So, here, in the very same chapter of Isaiah, we read that God *does* see us, even in our sins, and then we are told that, in spite of this, "[His] Spirit...will not depart".

That's an emphatic promise that, in spite of our sins, God says His Spirit will not be taken away from us, and in fact, this passage affirms that His Spirit remains on His people—even though they have sinned.

As always, we want to look at Jesus for the final word. He was the "exact representation of the Father" (Hebrews 1:3) and "the only one who has ever seen God" and he "came to reveal the Father to us." (See John 1:18)

What do we notice about Jesus? Does He, as God in the flesh, avert his gaze when surrounded by sinners? Not at all. Instead, those sinners are his closest friends. He spends so much time with them that the religious elite—who, by the way, were too holy to spend time with sinners—criticized him for it and called him a "friend of sinners" as an insult to His character. (See Matt. 11:19)

> WHAT DO WE NOTICE ABOUT JESUS? DOES HE, AS GOD IN THE FLESH, AVERT HIS GAZE WHEN SURROUNDED BY SINNERS? NOT AT ALL. INSTEAD, THOSE SINNERS ARE HIS CLOSEST FRIENDS.

So, is God really "too holy to look on our sin"?

Absolutely not! God's posture towards you is not disgust. God is not repulsed by your sins. God loves you. This is the dominant theme of the Gospels and the overwhelming message of Jesus: "For God so loved the World" (John 3:16)

So, you were created by love—because God *is* love—in the image of God—who is Love—which means *you are loved*. And, since nothing will ever separate you from His love (Romans 8:31–39), you will never know what it's like to *not* be loved by God, or to be separated from God's love.

Your eternal destiny is only to always and forever know more and more of God's endless love for you.

Our final question to answer regarding PSA theory is about Jesus substitutionary death for us upon the cross. This one might take a little longer to dig into, so let's do that in our next chapter.

CHAPTER 2

WAS JESUS OUR SUBSTITUTE?

"My own conviction, and that of the historic church, is that God was not punishing Jesus on the Cross at all... That is one reason I usually shy away from the language of substitution."

— BRAD JERSAK[1]

One of the central aspects of Calvin's "PSA" is that Christ became a substitute on our behalf, taking the punishment intended for us so that God's mercy, grace and forgiveness could be extended to humanity, once our sins were punished in Christ upon the cross.

Most of us seem to accept this idea instinctively, or at least have come to understand this perspective as an explanation of what was happening on the cross.

But is that the right way to think about the crucifixion of Christ? Is what Jesus did for us merely a substitution where Jesus stands in as a representative sacrifice?

I'm not so sure. In fact, the more I look into how the scriptures explain the mystery of the cross, the more I'm beginning to think that it was not so much a process of "substitution" as it was an outpouring of Christ's union with humanity.

In other words, I believe the real answers are more closely aligned with what's happening in the Incarnation of Christ and the deeper meaning of "God with us" as expressed in the Messianic title "Emmanuel."

As author Marcus Borg points out, the substitutionary theory of Jesus' death "was not central in the first thousand years of Christianity...[The] first systematic articulation of the cross as 'payment for sin' happened just over nine hundred years ago in 1098 in St. Anselm's treatise 'Cur Deus Homo?' [Why Did God Become Human?]"[2]

To be clear: In the substitutionary view, Jesus was our substitute on the cross because God demanded payment for our sins. Christ's death, then, was necessary because he had to die in our place—as our substitute—in order to pay our debt to God.

All of this is borrowed imagery from the Old Testament sacrificial system we see championed by Moses. But, while animals were sacrificed in the Old Covenant temple system, Borg argues that this "was not about payment for sin [but about] making something sacred by giving it as a gift to God, [because sacrifices were about] "thanksgiving, petition, purification, and reconciliation,"[3]—not substitution or payment.

Following Borg's train of thought, Richard Rohr adds:

"The metaphors of atonement, satisfaction, ransom, "paying the price," and "opening the gates," are just that—metaphors of transformation and transitioning. Too many theologians understood these in a transactional way instead of a transformational way."[4]

So, perhaps we need to take a step back and rethink the entire "substitutionary" and "payment" model of the atonement. Yes, this model has held sway over Christian thought for a thousand years now, but does it really line up with everything else being said about the cross in the New Testament? Are we missing something even more wondrous about the Incarnation, Crucifixion and Resurrection of Christ by settling for the mundane concepts of payment and substitution?

When Anselm developed his ideas about the cross, his intention was to provide a rational argument for the necessity of the incarnation and death of Jesus. But he was limited by his own capacity to see outside the boundaries of his assumptions. As Borg points out, Anselm based his atonement theory on:

> "...a cultural model drawn from his time and place: the relationship of a medieval lord to his peasants. If a peasant disobeyed the lord, could the lord simply forgive if he wanted to? No. Because that might imply that disobedience didn't matter that much. Instead, compensation must be made. Nothing less than the honor and order of the lord were at stake."[5]

Unfortunately, Anselm took his understanding of how lords relate to peasants and applied that to his model of how God relates to His children. This greatly skews the image of God as a loving Father who loves us and desires to restore us, heal us and transform us. Instead, it places God and all of humanity in a one-dimensional framework where the only thing that matters is God's honor and the need to punish us for our disobedience.

In Anselm's view, the problem then becomes mainly about payment, but this notion creates more than a few conundrums. First, if this need to repay God for our crimes is so important, how did the early Christians miss this fact for roughly a thousand years? Secondly, to whom do we owe this debt? If to God, then how does God pay the debt on our behalf through Christ? Why not simply forgive the debt as one might do whenever someone owes you something they cannot repay? Why, also, would we consider a debt as being "forgiven" if the person owed the sum actually receives what was due to them? Would that properly be considered "forgiveness"?

To summarize, Anselm developed his view based on the way he saw the world. Because the closest analogy to his mind was the medieval lord relating to one of his peasants, he saw things a certain way. But, we do not operate within the world of lords and peasants. We have other ways of seeing the world that might move us beyond a medieval perspective of God's nature and purpose.

So, if we remove our inherited substitutionary lenses, so to speak, what might we see? How might we approach the question of what Jesus was doing on the cross?

One way of doing this might be to look at what other theologian's ideas of the atonement were to see if they align closer to our understanding of Christ's character. For example, Franciscan John Duns Scotus (1266–1308) suggested that God did not *need* Jesus to die on the cross to love or forgive us. As Richard Rohr explains it, Scotus's view was that:

> "God's love was infinite from the first moment of creation; the cross was Love's dramatic portrayal in space and time. [He] built his argument on the pre-existent Cosmic Christ described in Colossians and Ephesians. Jesus is "the image of the invisible God" (Colossians 1:15) who came forward in a moment of time so we could look upon "the One we had pierced" (John 19:37) and see God's unconditional love for us, in spite of our failings.

> "Duns Scotus concluded that Jesus' death was not a substitution but a divine epiphany for all to see. Jesus was pure gift. The idea of gift is much more transformative than necessity, payment, or transaction. It shows that God is not violent, but loving. It is we who are violent...

> "The image of the cross was to change humanity, not a necessary transaction to change God—as if God needed changing! That, in a word, was the Franciscan nonviolent at-one-ment theory."[6]

So, in this view, God does not require a blood sacrifice as payment for our sins. God does not need anything to happen before we can be forgiven or loved or welcomed into His Divine presence. The crucifixion was necessary, not to change God's mind about us, but to change our minds about God.

THE CRUCIFIXION WAS NECESSARY, NOT TO CHANGE GOD'S MIND ABOUT US, BUT TO CHANGE OUR MINDS ABOUT GOD.

But, there still might be an even deeper and more profound way of understanding the cross that we haven't fully explored just yet. That perspective is rooted in the mystery and wonder of the Incarnation of Christ.

Many of us have an underdeveloped concept of the Incarnation. We see it primarily as something that Jesus did, but we fail to fully comprehend the implications of this miracle and what it says—not only about Christ but about us.

For example, when Christ took on flesh, he identified with humanity and became one with us. This means that Christ was not just one individual human being among other human beings on earth. Rather, it means that Christ, in the Incarnation, infused all of Creation with Himself, and all of Himself with Creation. Therefore, everything that happened to Christ happens to all of us, and everything experienced by us was shared in communion with Christ, and vice versa.

In 2 Peter we read that, because of Christ's identification with humanity, *"We have become partakers of the Divine nature."* (2 Peter 1:4) This means that when Jesus became a partaker of our Human nature, we also gained access to His Divine nature.

So, if we can carry this notion with us whenever we begin to examine the suffering of Christ on the cross of Cavalry, what we begin to see is that Jesus—who is in constant union with the Father and the Spirit—is also in constant union with us and all of humanity. This means that Jesus does not merely "substitute" himself *for* us. Instead, Christ suffers and dies *as* all of us.

The New Testament authors expressed it this way:

"For the love of Christ controls us, because we have concluded this: that one has died for all, therefore all have died; and he died for all…" (2 Corinthians 5:14–15)

"For if we have been united with him in a death like his, we shall certainly be united with him in a resurrection like his." (Romans 6:5)

"Now if we have died with Christ, we believe that we will also live with him." (Romans 6:8)

"Since the children have flesh and blood, [Christ] too shared in their humanity so that by his death he might break the power of him who holds the power of death—that is, the devil—and free those who all their lives were held in slavery by their fear of death." (Hebrews 2:14–15)

"But God, being rich in mercy, because of the great love with which he loved us, even when we were dead in our trespasses, made us alive together with Christ—by grace you have been saved—and raised us up with him and seated us with him in the heavenly places in Christ Jesus…" (Ephesians 2:4–6)

So, try to follow the train of thought here: Because Christ was literally the Incarnate God revealed in this miraculous union of God and Mankind, we are now also sharing in His experiences. Because He died, we died. Because He has been resurrected, we have been resurrected. Because Christ ascended to the right hand of the Father, we are also seated at the right hand of the Father in the heavenly places. Why? Because we are in Christ and Christ is in us.

Once we begin to grasp this concept, other verses begin to unfold for us like the petals of beautiful flower. Suddenly we can see ourselves and Christ intertwined in verses like these:

"For in him the whole fullness of deity dwells bodily, and you have been filled in him, who is the head of all rule and authority." (Colossians 2:9-10)

"And he put all things under his feet and gave him as head over all things to the church, which is his body, the fullness of him who fills all in all." (Ephesians 1:22-23)

This means that God did not punish Jesus on the cross for our sins. God suffered with Jesus on the cross. As Paul reminds us:

"God was in Christ reconciling the world to Himself, not counting our sins against us." (2 Corinthians 5:19)

We will have much more to say about this in later chapters. For now, let's try to clarify what we've learned so far:

The concept of Christ as substitute was not the view of the Christian Church for the first thousand years. It originated from Anselm who based the view on his observations of the relationship between medieval lords and peasants. Another way of looking at the atonement is to see it as something God does through Christ as One who stands in solidarity with humanity. Christ endures the cross, not instead of us, but as us; not as our substitute but as the God who is inseparably united with all humanity.

This view incorporates all of Christ's fullness into the equation. The atonement is not separated from the Incarnation. The crucifixion is not where God and man are at odds, but where God and all mankind are forever revealed as one and reconciled forever.

Now, let's be clear, even if Jesus was not suffering as a punishment for our sins; even if he did not stand as a substitute for us, there is one sense in which it could be said that Jesus *was* our substitute. As Brad Jersak explains:

"Did Jesus do for us what we could not do for ourselves? Of course he did. Did he 'step into the ring' as our substitute? Did he go through the battle royal with Satan, sin and death for us? Sure, he did. Did Jesus 'take a bullet for us'? Yes! The key is to remember, God is not the one holding the smoking gun. We are. And as he bleeds to death, he forgives us and says, 'I'll be back—see you in three days.'"[7]

So, to say that Jesus does what we could not do is a nuanced way of expressing this same notion of what was happening in the Incarnation, but without fully understanding or explaining "in what way" Christ accomplished this. This question is one we want to look into more closely, especially in light of how our union with God through Christ changes everything.

Before we do that, I think it's important to unpack what we mean when we say that Christ died for us and how Jesus subverts the Old Covenant Sacrificial system.

That's what we'll explore in our next chapter.

CHAPTER 3

WHAT DOES IT MEAN TO SAY CHRIST DIED FOR US?

"When Paul says that Jesus died for our sins, he adds the phrase 'according to the scriptures.' (1 Cor. 15:3) Now that doesn't mean, 'I can find three proof texts.' What it means is there is an entire scriptural narrative which is about the Creator God who is rescuing the world..."

— N.T. WRIGHT[1]

When we read in the Gospels or the writings of Paul that Jesus died for our sins, or that his blood was shed "for the forgiveness of sins," what does this mean? Our temptation is to go immediately to the Old Testament sacrificial system where an animal was laid upon the altar and it was put to death by the High Priest and the blood of that animal was somehow acceptable to God as a payment for our sins.

But, as we have already seen, this model isn't exactly the best way to see or understand the death of Christ. God never required these sacrificial rituals, nor did the blood of those animals take away anyone's sins. Now, certainly this is very likely how many Jewish Christians might have understood those terms. But this is precisely why the author of Hebrews goes to such great lengths to contrast what was required "under the Law" with what was accomplished through the Incarnation, Crucifixion and Resurrection of Christ. Yes, there were similarities, but quite often those similarities reveal the great chasm between the two Covenants. The one, older Covenant was fading and vanishing, and the other, newer Covenant was everlasting. In fact, it is precisely because there was something "*wrong*" with that older Covenant that a new Covenant was required.

> "But in fact the ministry Jesus has received is as superior to theirs as the covenant of which he is mediator is superior to the old one, since the new covenant is established on better promises. *For if there had been nothing wrong with that first covenant, no place would have been sought for another.*" (Hebrews 8:6–7, emphasis mine)

So, if Christ's death for us is not properly reflected in the sacrificial system of the Jewish Temple, then what's going on? How are we to think of it?

Before we answer that, I think we should look at the way the original disciples of Jesus—the Apostles in the book of Acts—talked about the cross. What did they say about the death of Jesus? Here are a few examples:

> "…this Man [Jesus], delivered over by the predetermined plan and foreknowledge of God, *you nailed to a cross by the hands of godless men and put Him to death.*" (Acts 2:23, emphasis mine)

> "…but [you] *put to death the Prince of life*, the one whom God raised from the dead, a fact to which we are witnesses." (Acts 3:15, emphasis mine)

> "The God of our fathers raised up Jesus, *whom you had put to death by hanging Him on a cross.*" (Acts 5:30, emphasis mine)

> "Which one of the prophets did your fathers not persecute? *They killed those who had previously announced the coming of*

the Righteous One, whose betrayers and murderers you have now become;" (Acts 7:52, emphasis mine)

Many Christians are surprised to read that the early Christians referred to the cross as the murder of an innocent man. It wasn't until much later that Christians started to talk about the cross as a beautiful act of God's love. For them, it was nothing less than an instrument of torture and death. The cross was where their friend and beloved Rabbi Jesus of Nazareth had been killed by those who hated and rejected him.

Why is this significant? Because it gives us a window into the brutality and ugliness of the cross. Yes, we can find profound examples of God's love and mercy when we examine the crucifixion of Christ, but let's not forget that a cross was originally an instrument of death used by the Romans to impose their rule over an occupied people with fear and dread.

It's also important for us to see that the Apostles did not ever communicate the cross as something that God did to Jesus. No. What we see is that the cross was what we did to Jesus. What God did was to raise him from the dead.

So, we might more accurately say—based on these verses from the book of Acts above—that Christ died *because* of our sins, more than he died "for our sins."

Today, after centuries of Calvin's PSA theory, we are conditioned to respond to this by saying that the reason Jesus died on the cross was because God required or demanded it. We might even be tempted to quote Isaiah 53:

"Yet it was the Lord's will to crush him and cause him to suffer, and though the Lord makes his life an offering for sin, he will see his offspring and prolong his days, and the will of the Lord will prosper in his hand." (Isaiah 53:10)

But what most of us don't realize is that this verse from Isaiah isn't accurate. In fact, this translation was added roughly a thousand years after the crucifixion of Jesus when the Masoretic Text of the Old Testament was created by Jewish Rabbis who intentionally changed certain passages that seemed to affirm that Jesus was the Messiah.

The version of the Old Testament, and therefore of this text from Isaiah, that was used during the time of Christ was the Greek Septuagint translation. It's also the version of the Hebrew Bible that Jesus and Paul actually read and quoted from. You'll notice that sometimes the quotations made in the Gospels or in Paul's epistles don't always match what is found in your Old Testament. That's because the version of the Old Testament used by most English translators is the newer Masoretic Text, not the older, more accurate Septuagint Text used by Jesus, Paul, and the other Apostles.

So, if you're curious what the Septuagint version of Isaiah 53:10 says, here's how it reads:

> "The Lord is willing to cleanse him of the injury. If you make a sin offering, our soul will see long-lived offspring, and the Lord is willing to remove him from the difficulty of his soul." (Isaiah 53:10)

Quite different, wouldn't you say? In this older, pre-altered version, it says that God was "willing to cleanse [the Messiah] of the injury", not that God was "pleased to crush him." It also says "if you make a sin offering", not that "the Lord makes his life an offering for sin." Once more, another huge difference where the entire meaning is twisted around to make God the one crushing Jesus, and God the one offering Jesus for our sins, which is nothing at all like what the original version suggests.

But this isn't the only passage that was drastically changed by the Rabbis in the Masoretic Text. Here are a few other examples for you:

- MASORETIC: "Surely he took up our pain and bore our suffering, yet we considered him punished by God, stricken by him, and afflicted." (Isaiah 53:4)

- SEPTUAGINT: "This one carries our sins and suffers pain for us, and we regarded him as one who is in difficulty, misfortune, and affliction." (Isaiah 53:4)

In the version of Isaiah read and quoted by Jesus it says that the Messiah was regarded as one who is in difficulty, misfortune and affliction. Later, the Jewish scribes edited the text to suggest that the Messiah was the one who was "…punished by God…"

- MASORETIC: "The Lord is a warrior; the Lord is his name." (Exodus 15:3)

- SEPTUAGINT: "The Lord who shatters wars, the Lord is his name." (Exodus 15:3)

So, is God a warrior as the more modern text says, *or* is God the one who "shatters wars" as the original version says?

In Romans 9:33, Paul quotes Isaiah 28:16 from the Septuagint which refers to Jesus as the cornerstone which God has placed in Zion, saying "whoever believes in Him will not be put to shame." However, in the Masoretic text the stone is not a person in whom one should trust but a promise from God that, if one believes in the promise, "…will not panic."

In Romans 10:15, when Paul quotes Isaiah 52:7 from the Septuagint it actually proclaims *"the good news"* [or "gospel"] message. But, in the Masoretic text it does not announce good news or gospel, but merely "peace."

In Romans 10:20, Paul reads from the Septuagint version of Isaiah 65:1–2 and quotes that "...God is found by people who did not look for Him." This is an obvious reference to the Gentiles. However, in the Masoretic text it was changed to say that God is ready for Israel to find Him, with no mention of the Gentiles.

In Acts 15:16–18, James [the brother of Jesus] quotes from Amos 9:11–12. This quote is from the Septuagint and freely welcomes other nations to seek the Lord. However, the Masoretic text changes that to say that the house of David (or the House of Israel) will possess the nations, which completely undermines the meaning of the point that James is trying to make.

In Romans 10:21, Paul once again quotes from the Septuagint version of Isaiah 11:10 which makes reference to "the One who rises to rule." However, in the Masoretic text these words have been removed entirely.

That's the short list. But, hopefully you can see the problem with quoting from the Masoretic Text versus the Septuagint Text, especially when it comes to verses that have been changed to undermine the scriptures as read and quoted by Jesus, Paul and the other disciples.

THAT IS THE SHAME OF THE CROSS. WE PUT THE INNOCENT SON OF GOD TO DEATH. BUT GOD RAISED HIM TO LIFE AGAIN.

So, the entire point we should take away from this lengthy examination of texts is this: It *did not* please the Lord to crush His Son on the cross. God was not the one doing the crushing, we were. That is the shame of the cross. We put the innocent Son of God to death. But God raised Him to life again.

As author Baxter Kruger says, "It was not the wrath of the Father that was poured out on Jesus at Calvary, but the wrath of the human race. Jesus and the Gospels are clear and emphatic."[2]

The evidence from scripture on this point is abundant:

"Behold, we are going up to Jerusalem, and the Son of Man will be delivered up to the chief priests and scribes, and they will condemn Him to death, and will deliver Him up to the Gentiles to mock and scourge and crucify Him, and on the third day He will be raised up." (Matthew 20:18–19)

"For He was teaching His disciples and telling them, "The Son of Man is to be delivered up into the hands of men, and they will kill Him; and when He has been killed, He will rise again three days later." (Mark 9:31)

"And He took the twelve aside and said to them, "Behold, we are going up to Jerusalem, and all things which are written through the prophets about the Son of Man will be accomplished. For He will be delivered up to the Gentiles, and will be mocked and mistreated and spit upon, and after they have scourged Him, they will kill Him; and the third day He will rise again." (Luke 18:31–33)

"They therefore cried out, "Away with Him, away with Him, crucify Him!" Pilate said to them, "Shall I crucify your King?" The chief priests answered, "We have no king but Caesar." And so he then delivered Him up to them to be crucified. They took Jesus therefore, and He went out, bearing His own cross, to the place called the Place of a Skull… There they crucified Him… (John 19:15–18)

The only wrath that put Jesus on that cross came from humanity, not from the Father.

We've already talked about how the sacrifice Jesus made in the Incarnation when he humbled himself and took the form of a servant—not as a disguise but as an unveiling of the true nature of God; the One who comes not to be served but to serve. (See Philippians 2 and Mark 10:45)

We've also talked about how the author of Hebrews affirms that God's will had nothing to do with sacrifice or bloodshed, and how there were numerous examples in the Old Testament of how God freely forgave sins without the shedding of blood.

We've also seen how Jesus always forgave everyone he encountered, no matter what. He never waited to be asked for forgiveness, nor did he demand any confession of sins in advance of extending forgiveness. Jesus simply forgave, and since he only does what he sees the Father doing, this is what God does in response to our sins: He forgives.

We've seen that the "wrath of God" is often a reflection of our own wrathfulness, not a true picture of the heart of God as revealed in Christ.

Finally, we've talked about how the Incarnation of Christ testified to a union between God and Man that transcends the physical body of Jesus and points to an abiding unity between flesh and Spirit; God and Humankind.

So, with all of that in mind, let's take another look at the cross of Christ. If we do, what we'll see is that God was in Christ suffering the wrath of humanity. We killed Jesus. God did not. His response was to answer the prayer of Jesus— *"Father, forgive them for they know not what they do"*—as He endured the cross along with His Son.

Everett Ferguson, in his book *The Church of Christ,* makes an astounding observation that needs to be considered:

> "In the New Testament, instead of a sacrifice offered by human beings to God, [the hilaskomai] word group refers to a sacrifice made by God himself (Romans 3:25; 1 John 4:10). Some passages use the expected language of a sacrifice offered to God (Ephesians 5:2), but the New Testament usage of hilasterion and hilasmos stands the pagan Greek idea on its head. God is not appeased or propitiated. He himself acts to remove the sin that separates human beings from him. Instead of humans offering the sacrifice, God himself expiates or makes atonement for sins. God performs the sacrifice. The divine action for

human salvation completely reverses the usual understanding of religion and worship."[3]

This means that Jesus completely subverts the entire sacrificial system. Under that old model, the people offered their sacrifices on the altar to appease the wrath of an angry god. But on the cross, we see a loving God who offers Himself to appease the wrath of His people.

UNDER THE OLD MODEL, NO ONE WAS EVER SAVED OR FORGIVEN, BUT UNDER THE RADICAL NEW MODEL OF CHRIST, EVERYONE IS SAVED, HEALED, TRANSFORMED AND FOREVER MADE WHOLE. "IT IS FINISHED!"

Under the old model, no one was ever saved or forgiven, but under the radical new model of Christ, everyone is saved, healed, transformed and forever made whole. "It is finished!"

Jesus not only turns the entire thing inside-out, he brings an end to sacrifice forever. (See Dan. 9:27; Rom. 10:4)

So, yes, the Apostle Paul is correct when he reminds us that "Christ died…according to the Scriptures" (1 Corinthians 15:3), but in this case our English translations often mislead us. When we look at what that verse says in the Greek with fresh eyes, as New Testament scholar David Bentley Hart has endeavored to do in his most recent translation of this passage, we see this:

> "For, among the very first things, I delivered to you what I had also received: that the Anointed [Christ] *died because of our sins*, in accord with the scriptures…" (1 Corinthians 15:3, DBH Translation)

This sheds new light on our understanding of the cross and what the crucifixion was really all about, doesn't it? Now we can see that Christ's death was "because of our sins" and not "for our sins." In other words, it was our sin that murdered Christ. We crucified Jesus. God forgave us of that sin, because that is what God does. God forgives.

In the Incarnation, Jesus took on flesh and this was not merely his own personal humanity. It was a symbol of God's solidarity with all of mankind. In Christ we see both God and humanity at once.

As Brad Jersak puts it:

> "Christ did not just take on an individual human nature of his own. Christ assumed human nature (all of humanity), so that 'as in Adam, all...so in Christ, all.' He united with all in his birth and life so that he united with all in his death and resurrection... in rising, he raises all humanity with himself."[4]

The glorious reality for us now that Christ has made possible through his complete fulfillment of the Law and the transformation of humanity through Himself—is that we are "new creations...the old has gone, behold all things have been made new!" (2 Corinthians 5:17)

SO, IT'S NOT SO MUCH THAT CHRIST DIED FOR US AS IT IS THAT CHRIST DIED AS US—IN UNION WITH US AND WITH THE FATHER AND THE SPIRIT—AND THAT IN HIS DYING ALL DIED, AND IN HIS RISING ALL WERE RAISED INTO NEWNESS OF LIFE WITH CHRIST

The crucial reality of the Incarnation is this: Jesus and Humanity are one, in the very same way that Jesus and the Father are one. To deny one, is in fact, to deny the other. Either Jesus and the Father are one, and therefore Jesus and humanity or one, *or* Jesus is not one with the Father, and they are not one with us.

For, as Jesus tells us: "In that day you shall know that I am in My Father, and you in Me, and I in you" (John 14:20)

In Christ we find the oneness of Father and Son, and the Oneness of God and mankind, all at once. These truths are intertwined with one another, even as we are intertwined with Christ, who is in the Father as we are in Christ, who is in us all.

So, it's not so much that Christ died *for* us as it is that Christ died *as* us—in union with us and with the Father and the Spirit—and that in His dying all died, and in His rising all were raised into newness of life with Christ, because of that unbreakable union between God and man; Christ and us.

As author and theologian Baxter Kruger explains:

> "His oneness with his Father and the Holy Spirit, and his oneness with us in our humanity in darkness and with creation in its brokenness, form the non-negotiable reality that we ignore to our peril. Jesus' very existence is 'the ground and grammar of theology,' both the possibility and the inner logic of authentic thought about God and divine relations with humanity. We dare not say a word to anybody anywhere that betrays this Jesus Christ and the reality established in him. Failure here is not simply a theological mistake; it is to consign ourselves to ourselves. It is to limit our hearts to try to thrive on our own speculation. And no matter how we dress it up with solemn religious words spoken in hushed tones while wearing holy vestments, speculation is speculation, always devoid of authority, vacuous of weight before the hurting soul."[5]

Or, to put it another way: "Christ is all, and in all" (Colossians 3:11) and because of this truth, the crucifixion was God's subversive plan to transform our wrath against Him, and His Son, into the means of our liberation, reconciliation and salvation from the bondage of sin and death.

We are all, together, vicariously co-crucified with Christ—and the Father, and the Spirit—and in that union with God on the cross, we are all set free and partakers of the Divine Nature. (2 Peter 1:4)

Here's how Ephesians describes this subversive plan that God brilliantly devised to rescue us from ourselves:

> "As for you, you were dead in our transgressions and sins, in which you used to live when you followed the ways of this world and of the ruler of the kingdom of the air...All of us also lived

among them at one time, gratifying the cravings of our sinful nature and following its desires and thoughts. Like the rest, we were by nature children of ire, but because of His great love for us, God, who is rich in mercy, made us alive with Christ even when we were dead in our transgressions..." (Ephesians 2:1–5)

In this verse, we see how cleverly God catapulted us from death into life.

Here's how it works: First, God knew that we were dead in our sins. He saw clearly how we thought and how our actions were motivated by our selfish desires. Like tossing red meat into a school of sharks, God sent His Anointed One into this sea of humanity. What else could happen? As with the prophets that came before Jesus, we turned on Him and put Him to death. Just exactly as He knew we would.

But, notice what happened next: *"Because of His great love for us, God...made us alive with Christ..."*

Even when we kill the Author of Life, He responds with great love. Rather than respond with wrath, God forgives and restores us. When Christ dies and descends into the bowels of death, this ignites the resurrection power to *"make us alive with Christ, even when we were dead in our transgressions."*

Notice that this only works if we are in union with Christ already. Because we were made "alive with Christ even when we were dead in our transgressions", which is only possible if we *were already* one with Christ. Without this oneness between us and the Father, and between Jesus and the Father, none of this would have happened.

Paul concludes this by saying:

"And God raised us up with Christ and seated us with Him in the heavenly realms in Christ Jesus, in order that in the coming ages He might demonstrate to everyone the incomparable riches of His grace, expressed in His kindness to us in Christ Jesus." [v. 6–7]

Do you see how much He loves you? Can you believe how far He is willing to go to make you His own?

Isn't it incredible? He has taken our wrath and transformed it into our salvation. He has taken death and remade it into a catalyst for life. Because of this, we are healed, we are made alive, and we are resurrected with Christ as new creatures in Him.

As we take some time to allow this glorious reality to settle deeper into our hearts and permeate our minds and transform us from the inside out, let's prepare ourselves for the next chapter. This will be our opportunity to examine the question, "What is sin?" and what does it really mean for us to "miss the mark"?

CHAPTER 4

MISSING THE MARK ON MISSING THE MARK

"If it is from Christ that we are to learn how God relates himself to sin, suffering, evil, and death, it would seem that he provides us little evidence of anything other than a regal, relentless, and miraculous enmity: sin he forgives, suffering he heals, evil he casts out, and death he conquers."

— DAVID BENTLEY HART[1]

Most Christians are well-acquainted with the verse that reminds us of our sinful nature:

"For all have sinned and fallen short of the glory of God." (Romans 3:23)

But what does all of that really mean? Well, we know that the Greek word *"Hamartia"* in this verse for "sinned" refers to shooting an arrow and missing the target. So, we often say that sin is to "miss the mark" in the sense that the "mark" is total perfection.

Therefore, since we all fail to be perfect or "sinless", then we are all doomed. But I think that's the wrong way to think of it.

Here's why: Would it be sinful for a giraffe to fall short of an ability to read French? Would it be sinful if an otter couldn't play guitar? Of course not. But why? Because reading French isn't something any giraffe can do. Otters are not capable of playing guitar. Therefore, it's not "missing the mark" if they can't do those things.

Looking at the verse in Romans about sin as "missing the mark" again might help:

> "For all have sinned and fallen short of the glory of God." (Romans 3:23)

So, what is "the glory of God" that we have fallen short of?

This is the key question. If we look at references to "the glory of God" in the scriptures we'll see early on this amazing verse in Exodus:

> "I cry out to you with everything that is in me: *show me your glory*, ...God answered his cry and revealed His glory to him [Moses], And God said, "I Myself will make all my goodness pass before you and will proclaim my Name before you; and I will be gracious to whom I will be gracious, and will show compassion to whom I will show compassion." (Exodus 33:18–19, emphasis mine)

Or, to put it another way, when Moses cried out to see the glory of God, what God showed Moses was His goodness, His graciousness and His compassion. That is the "glory of God" that Moses saw.

So, if the Glory of God is essentially the goodness, grace and mercy of God, then if we have fallen short of the glory of God we have simply

> WOULD IT BE SINFUL FOR A GIRAFFE TO FALL SHORT OF AN ABILITY TO READ FRENCH? WOULD IT BE SINFUL IF AN OTTER COULDN'T PLAY GUITAR? OF COURSE NOT. BUT WHY? BECAUSE READING FRENCH ISN'T SOMETHING ANY GIRAFFE CAN DO.

failed to be like God —full of goodness, kindness, grace and mercy towards others.

That's a far cry from being "perfect", isn't it?

Now, if you're still not convinced, I need to show you how Jesus also redefines God's Holiness in the very same way.

One of the most fundamental disagreements between Jesus and the Pharisees had to do with how they viewed God, and this influenced how they understood Holiness.

For the Pharisees, Holiness was a very strict code. It had everything to do with how they viewed God —Powerful, aloof, set apart and much too Holy and perfect to even glance towards anyone who was a sinner.

Because of this view of God, the Pharisees behaved in much the same way: Too godly to associate with sinners and too focused on keeping Holiness codes to bother with the lives of those dirty, filthy commoners who didn't observe the Law as perfectly as they did.

Holiness, as the Pharisees understood and practiced it, had everything to do with being good, godly and perfect, and therefore "set apart" from those who were on the outside. By definition, this understanding of Holiness created an "Us vs Them" separation from God and the unclean; and between them and the sinners around them.

But Jesus took a very different approach to this concept. He seems to have prioritized compassion and love over Holiness and perfection. This is why we see Jesus spending so much time with "sinners" who were not acceptable to the Pharisees; the drunkards, the prostitutes, the sick, the outcasts, and the Roman-sympathizing tax collectors from within their own faith community.

Some have noted that Jesus seems to favor compassion while the Pharisees appear to prefer Holiness, but I disagree. I think that what we see is that Jesus and the Pharisees both prioritized Holiness, but the difference was that they just had very different definitions of what Holiness was and wasn't.

As I've pointed out, the Pharisees understood Holiness as being "above" or "set apart" from the unholiness of those who did not observe the Law. It was a very divisive, exclusive and elite view of Holiness that, by definition, required an "In" or "Out" policy that was very black and white.

The Pharisees justified this behavior and view on what they believed was a very clear picture of God from their Scriptures. God was "high and lifted up" and no man was worthy to look upon God and live because of our sinfulness and wretched condition. Especially as compared to the unimaginable glory and perfection of Almighty God who was surrounded night and day by the Holy angels upon His eternal throne set far above the heavens.

But Jesus took a different approach. Jesus saw God as being full of mercy and compassion. He had plenty of scripture verses to back that up, by the way. But he also pressed this perspective about the absolute love of God for all mankind as his basis for why we should strive to be just like God; showing mercy and love to sinners and saints alike.

This is especially telling when Jesus commands his disciples to "love your enemies" in his Sermon on the Mount, simply because this is what God does! In fact, Jesus tells us that God brings rain on the just and the unjust alike—in total contradiction to something Moses said in Deuteronomy—and makes that his basis for why we should also show love to the righteous and the unrighteous.

And then, guess what Jesus says after this? He says: "Be holy, even as your heavenly Father is holy." (Matthew 5:48)

This is a direct shot across the bow of the Pharisees who had taught that being holy as God is holy meant setting yourself apart from sinners and not associating with those who were unclean. Jesus turns the entire thing on its head and says:" This is what it means to be Holy—being like God. And what is God like? God is merciful and loving to everyone—even to those who hate Him! Therefore, you should be Holy the way God is Holy, and that means showing love to everyone!"

THIS IS WHAT IT MEANS TO BE HOLY—BEING LIKE GOD. AND WHAT IS GOD LIKE? GOD IS MERCIFUL AND LOVING TO EVERYONE—EVEN TO THOSE WHO HATE HIM!

So, that phrase: *"Be Holy even as your Heavenly Father is Holy"* is not a statement about being perfect, and it's not a challenge for us to do the impossible. Instead, it's a redefinition of what Holiness is all about—loving as God loves—not about dividing ourselves from one another over who is more perfect or godly than someone else.[2]

Jesus redefines Holiness for us and sets the Pharisees back on their heels.

Whenever we separate ourselves from others because they are sinful, we are deceived as the Pharisees were about what Holiness is all about.

Whenever we create an Us vs Them division between ourselves and others, we are following the Pharisees playbook.

But, if we can learn to see Holiness the way Jesus sees it—as being like God—then we can learn to see that God is love and loving like God does is what makes us Holy.

Once you understand that Jesus redefined the Holiness of God, or "being perfect as God is perfect" as something equal to expressing kindness and compassion to everyone, even our enemies, it all makes sense.

Bible scholar and author N.T. Wright agrees:

"Sin is a failure rather than simply the breaking of rules. *It's the failure to be genuinely human.* The Greek word "Hamartia" refers to shooting an arrow and missing the target. *What is the target? The target is genuine humanness. What is genuine humanness? It's reflecting God's image. Whenever we are tempted to sin, what is actually going on is that there is something we're supposed to be doing and being to honor God in the world and in our family and in our own lives, and sin is what draws away from that.*" (emphasis mine)[3]

Putting all these ideas together, we can see that "falling short of the glory of God" is not failure to be sinless. It's not a failure to be perfect. Rather, it's a failure to express the goodness, kindness, mercy and grace of God to one another.

In other words, it's not a sin for a giraffe to fail at algebra, but it IS a sin for a giraffe to fail at being the giraffe she was always intended to be.

To put it another way, it's not a sin for us to fail at perfect sinlessness —because that's impossible. But it *is* a sin to miss the mark of being Christlike as we were created to be.

When I first saw this truth, I was discussing it online with a group of friends and one of them, Amy Chumbley, said this: *"What if we are the glory of God?"*

We all had to stop and catch our breath as she said it. Slowly it started to sink in.

TO PUT IT ANOTHER WAY, IT'S NOT A SIN FOR US TO FAIL AT PERFECT SINLESSNESS —BECAUSE THAT'S IMPOSSIBLE. BUT IT IS A SIN TO MISS THE MARK OF BEING CHRISTLIKE AS WE WERE CREATED TO BE.

She was right. We are all created in the image of God. God is love. Therefore, we are all intended to reflect the glory of God—our identity in Christ—and whenever we fall short of that, then we've failed to live up to our true self; our true nature, as children of God.

Then it just kept getting better. Hours later the group kept messaging one another and posting in the private Facebook group thinks like:

> "And we all, who with unveiled faces contemplate the Lord's glory, are being transformed into his image with ever-increasing glory, which comes from the Lord, who is the Spirit." (2 Corinthians 3:18)

> "I have given them the glory you gave me, that they may be one as we are one." (John 17:22)

And then one friend posted this:

> "The other cool thing about this is, about two weeks ago, I texted a friend and asked them "what does that even mean, the Glory of the Lord." I was kinda asking it in somewhat of a snarky manner, not towards him, but just in general, as in so many "movements" the Glory of the Lord is prophesied, and honestly, it's like it has become a catch phrase for certain evangelical prophetic movements (I could name so many). I was fed up with it back then and for some reason it sickens me when I hear it now because it just means NOTHING. It feels empty and pointless. BUT THIS.... that WE are God's Glory, it is sooooo life giving and compassionate. I was driving through a Walmart parking lot and I saw a lady, and it hit me "She IS the glory of the Lord" It's just healing and will help me with people I struggle with, also."

And then another friend said:

> "...because Christ has forgiven our sins, we are now free to be who we were always created to be in Christ—sons and daughters of God who reflect the glory of God by the ways we show love and mercy and grace and compassion!"

And that inspired someone else to say:

> "What if sin is simply unbelief in the love God has for us? If repentance is changing the mind, then what if sin is having thoughts that need to be changed? God woos us into His Love. It's on Him/Her just as it is our responsibility as parents

to reassure our love to our children. I'm handing the "bow [and arrow]" to Him now!"

After this exchange, I went back and took another look at Romans 3 and what I saw there was a long list of things we have all done in our sinfulness, but that list was the exact opposite of the "glory of God" we are all called to manifest: love, kindness, compassion and mercy.

So, while we may have—in the past—fallen short of this glory of God, the good news is that now, because Christ has removed our sins from us forever, we are all capable of reflecting the glory of God in our lives today!

We are not "sinners" but children who reflect the glory of God our Father.

So, rather than focus on being sinless—which isn't even the goal or the point of this passage—we can, instead, focus on being the beloved children of God who are now empowered to fully reflect the glory of God by producing the fruit of love, joy, peace, patience, kindness, gentleness and self-control.

Or to put it another way, we are not giraffes failing to speak French. We are not sinners failing to reach some perfect state of sinlessness. We are children of God who are learning to reflect the glory of God by simply resting in the fact that we are God's children and God is our loving Father. We are learning to abide in this reality so that our lives can fully reflect God's glory.

There was a time when we saw sin as missing the mark of perfection the way an archer misses a target that is a thousand miles away and behind a tree. Today, we might more properly understand that missing the mark and "falling short of the glory of God" is more about our failure to be who we already are in Christ.

This means that taking up the bow and arrow now simply means learning to rest and abide in Christ. It means learning to realize my identity is based on the fact that I am one who is already loved, valued and treasured by God—and so is everyone else.

This means I can begin to produce the good fruit of love, joy, peace, patience, kindness, gentleness and self-control as I abide in Christ.

There was a time when we fell short of this glory. But that time is

> IN OTHER WORDS, OUR SINS LEAD US TO DEATH, BUT IT IS NOT GOD WHO DOES THE KILLING, IT IS THE SIN ITSELF.

past. Today we are among those who understand that God is Love and all who live in Love live in God and God lives in them.

This is good news, my friends. This is very, very good news.

But we're still not done rethinking this question of sin. Not yet. There are just a few more things we need to understand before we move on.

THE WAGES OF SIN?

One of the most common verses we turn to when we think about sin is found in Romans 6:23 where we read:

"The wages of sin is death…"

But we need to ask if this death comes because God is the one who takes our life? Is this a statement about how we have broken the law and now God has no choice but to exact our just punishment for the infraction? Or, could it be that this verse is simply saying that sin carries its own reward like a deadly contagion that is spread through direct contact?

In other words, our sins lead us to death, but it is not God who does the killing, it is the sin itself.

If so, perhaps this is why God often warns us to avoid sin, because He loves us and wants us to live and not die. Perhaps this is more consistent with how a good Father would treat the children that He loved so dearly. Not killing His children when they fall short, but warning them to avoid those things that might harm them and working to restore them when they suffer as a result.

Taking another look at that verse from Romans we see that there's a lot more going on than merely a statement about how deadly sin can be:

> "The wages of sin is death, but the gift of God is eternal life through Jesus Christ our Lord." (Romans 6:23)

This is the entire story. Sin brings death, but God is the One who gives us the free gift of life through Jesus Christ. God is not the One killing people. He's the One giving them the free gift of eternal life through Christ.

Jesus says almost exactly the same thing.

> "The thief comes only to steal and kill and destroy; I have come that they may have life, and have it to the full." (John 10:10)

So, it is not God who responds to our sins with death. His response is life, forgiveness, mercy and reconciliation.

BEHOLD THE LAMB OF GOD WHO KEEPS REMINDING US OF OUR SINS?

A few years ago, we met a woman who told us that her spiritual gift was to look at people and see their sins. "It's like all of their sins are just written across their face," she said. This "gift" kept her from fully experiencing the joy of community within the Body of Christ. All she could see was sin, no matter where she looked.

So many Christian churches today are continually fixated on how sinful we all are. They constantly remind us that we are unworthy and that our sins are filthy and that these things keep us separated from God. But then, in the very same breath, they will remind us that Jesus is "the Lamb of God who takes away the sins of the World."

So, which is it? I mean, if the Good News of the Gospel is that we were sinners and Christ's death sets us free from the Law of Sin and Death, then why are we still wallowing in our sinfulness?

And if we are still enslaved to our sinfulness, then how can we proclaim that Jesus took away our sins and nailed them once and for all to the cross?

Are we really set free from the Law of Sin and Death? Did Jesus actually take away our sins and nail them to the cross once and for all?

Or, are we just hopeless sinners who can never, ever, truly be set free from our filthy sinfulness?

What about verses that challenge this notion? Like the one—which almost never gets quoted by these same sin-obsessed Christians—that tells us:

> "...that in Christ God was reconciling the World to Himself, *not counting our sins against us,* and entrusting us with this message of reconciliation." (2 Corinthians 5:19)

So, sometimes I wonder if we need to keep people in a constant state of limbo between being loved/accepted and condemned/ashamed in order to perpetuate a religious system of control. If so, then a continual emphasis on our sinfulness is required to accomplish this. Because once you start setting people free—really free—from the shame and guilt of their sins it can be really hard to grow a religious movement.

See, if everyone is always wondering whether or not they are free, there's always a reason for them to come back again next week to find out. And, if our reconciliation with God is in doubt, or in flux, then we'll always need someone to reassure us that this forgiveness is available—at least as long as we remain members in good standing with the church and keep paying our tithes.

Now, imagine the chaos if everyone actually *knew* for a fact that they were—right now—totally and completely forgiven and absolutely reconciled to God. (No, seriously. Imagine it.)

What if our message to everyone was simply this: *"God loves you. God isn't counting your sins against you anymore. God has reconciled you completely. You are forgiven. Totally forgiven. You are accepted. Completely. You are God's beloved child. When you're ready to come home, God is waiting for you with arms wide open."*

How beautiful would that be?

So, why do we emphasize our sinfulness and downplay our message of reconciliation in favor of a story about how broken and miserable we are? Maybe because this message tends to keep us coming back for more.

WHAT DEFINES OUR CHARACTER AND OUR IDENTITY IS BASED ON WHOSE IMAGE WE ARE ALL MADE IN. WHAT DEFINES OUR VALUE AND OUR WORTH IS CALCULATED BY THE PRICE SOMEONE IS WILLING TO PAY TO BE WITH US FOREVER.

Now, I can already hear some of you saying: "But Keith, we *are* sinners! Everyone sins!"

Yes, that is true. We all make mistakes. We all fall short of the Glory of God.

But that is not our identity. That is not who we *are*.

We are the children of God. We are beloved. We are reconciled.

One could make the case that everyone on the planet defecates. We all poop. *But is that who we are?* Are we, at the core of our being, "Poopers?" Does this daily, repetitive movement define our character or reflect our identity? No. It does not.

What defines our character and our identity is based on whose image we are all made in. What defines our value and our worth is calculated by the price someone is willing to pay to be with us forever.

God has said that we are worth dying for. God has demonstrated our value by paying the ultimate price to be with us. God has declared that we are all made in the image of the Divine. God has, in Christ, reconciled the entire World completely and does not count our sins against us. So, let us "behold, the Lamb of God who [really does] take away the sins of the World!"

FINAL THOUGHTS

Remember that woman I mentioned earlier? The one who said her spiritual gift was to look at people and see their sins? Well, that night, sitting in my living room, I believe the Holy Spirit inspired me to respond to her with just the right perspective and I want to share it with all of you, too, because I think this might really help us to break out of our focus on sins.

Here's what I told her:

"If you're looking for my sins you'll find them. Believe me. I could give you a list of things as long as my leg if you want it. The truth is, we could all go around the room and share our sins with one another. But, if we spend all of our time together focused on our sins, what sort of fellowship would we really have together?

"Now, imagine if we spent our time looking for Christ in one another. Wouldn't that be better? Because here's the truth: Whatever you're looking for is what you'll find. So, if you look for my sins, or anyone else's sins, you'll find plenty to keep you busy. But, if you start looking for Christ in one another, you'll start to see that, too! And then imagine if we all started to look for Christ in one another. Then imagine what it would be like if we started to call it out? "Hey brother, I see Christ in you!" or "Hey sister, your face is radiating the love of Christ right now!" Imagine how great that would be!"

This is my advice to all of us: Stop looking for sin. Stop focusing on the thing you have been set free from. Stop counting your sins. Stop evaluating everyone else's sins. Instead, start focusing on God who is love. Start looking for His love in others. Start pointing it out when you see it: "I see the love of God in you!" or "The way you show compassion for others is so Christlike!"

The glorious reality of God's presence is alive inside of you, my friends. God and the Son have come to make their home in you by the power of the Holy Spirit. Nothing will ever separate you from this amazing love of God that is higher, wider, longer and deeper than any of us could ever imagine. It transcends knowledge.

You are loved with an everlasting love. Focus on this. Your sins are washed away. They have been cast as far away as the East is from the West. God remembers them no more. You have been reconciled to God. Why not meditate on this?

ADDENDUM: LAST THOUGHTS ON SIN

I promise, this will be the last thing I have to say about sin. But, it's too good to pass up.

Just take a moment to read Romans 5 and starting with verse 12, please notice the flow of Paul's argument here. In light of everything we've learned so far, I think it might really bless you:

> "Therefore, just as sin entered the world through one man, and death through sin, and in this way death came to all people, because all sinned—

"To be sure, sin was in the world before the law was given, but sin is not charged against anyone's account where there is no law. Nevertheless, death reigned from the time of Adam to the time of Moses, even over those who did not sin by breaking a command, as did Adam, who is a pattern of the one to come.

"But the gift is not like the trespass. For if the many died by the trespass of the one man, how much more did God's grace and the gift that came by the grace of the one man, Jesus Christ, overflow to the many! Nor can the gift of God be compared with the result of one man's sin: The judgment followed one sin and brought condemnation, but the gift followed many trespasses and brought justification. For if, by the trespass of the one man, death reigned through that one man, how much more will those who receive God's abundant provision of grace and of the gift of righteousness reign in life through the one man, Jesus Christ!

"Consequently, just as one trespass resulted in condemnation for all people, so also one righteous act resulted in justification and life for all people. For just as through the disobedience of the one man the many were made sinners, so also through the obedience of the one man the many will be made righteous.

"The law was brought in so that the trespass might increase. But where sin increased, grace increased all the more, so that, just as sin reigned in death, so also grace might reign through righteousness to bring eternal life through Jesus Christ our Lord." (NIV, emphasis mine)

CHAPTER 5

WORM-FREE CHRISTIANITY

"In conservative Christianity you are told you are unacceptable. You are judged with regard to your relationship to God. Thus you can only be loved positionally, not essentially. And, contrary to any assumed ideal of Christian love, you cannot love others for their essence either. This is the horrible cost of the doctrine of original sin."

— MARLENE WINELL[1]

"Amazing Grace, how sweet the sound, that saved a wretch like me."

— JOHN NEWTON (1725–1807)

Over the years I've become painfully aware of an undercurrent within Christianity that I call "Worm Theology." This is the pervasive assumption that is constantly reinforced from a variety of sources that you and I are essentially nothing but worthless, filthy, unlovable creatures that God only manages to tolerate through an enormous outpouring of Grace.

It is expressed in our hymns and worship songs when we sing in unison about how we are "not worthy" of God's love or harmonize together about how God "saved a wretch like me."

It's also overtly stated in our doctrinal statements of faith, repeated in our Bible Studies, affirmed in our Sunday sermons and reiterated endlessly in our conversations with one another.

It goes something like this: *We are scum. There is nothing good in me. My mind and my heart are deceitfully wicked. We are not worthy of God's love. We do not deserve anything other than God's wrath.*

> **THIS IS WORM THEOLOGY. AND THE REASON WHY IT BOTHERS ME SO MUCH IS THAT IT'S A DIRECT CONTRADICTION TO EVERYTHING JESUS CAME TO REVEAL TO US ABOUT WHO WE REALLY ARE AND WHO GOD REALLY IS.**

This is worm theology. And the reason why it bothers me so much is that it's a direct contradiction to everything Jesus came to reveal to us about who we really are and who God really is.

In other words, if we blindly accept the notion that we are unworthy of God's love—that we are worms and wretches—then the way we relate to God will always be colored by this assumption. We will start to accept that this is how God sees us. We will begin to believe that this is who we are. We will beg, and grovel, and wallow in our sinfulness and always feel that God looks at us with complete disappointment and disgust.

Martin Luther was the first to say that, to God, we are like snow-covered dung and once said this about himself:

> "I am the ripe shit; so also is the world a wide asshole; then shall we soon part."[2]

Now, that might be offensive to you. If so, I apologize. It's offensive to me, too. Not so much for the choice of words as for the idea that it communicates: that to God we are nothing but excrement and the entire world is nothing but a disgusting source of endless filth.

This is not who we are. It's not how God sees us. We should never embrace this line of thinking or entertain such notions about ourselves, or about God.

There are no worms in the Body of Christ.

Now, the songs we sing on Sunday morning might suggest otherwise. We may love to sing about the love of God and how "I couldn't earn it, I don't deserve it…", but this isn't ever the way God speaks about His love for us.

Just as no loving parent would ever look their child in the eye and say, "I love you so much, but you don't deserve my love, and you could never earn this love I have for you."

Now, what we might say as a loving parent is something like: "You don't need to earn my love, and you don't have to deserve it." Why? Because we love them already! The love we have for our children isn't about earning or deserving. It just is. That's what matters.

The truth is this: once we understand who we are in Christ, we begin to step into our identity as new creatures who are partakers of the Divine nature. We are not "worms" or "wretches" who are in need of God's constant pity, nor are we objects of God's disgust or disappointment. We are sons and daughters of God. We are loved and treasured.

THE TRUTH IS THIS: ONCE WE UNDERSTAND WHO WE ARE IN CHRIST, WE BEGIN TO STEP INTO OUR IDENTITY AS NEW CREATURES WHO ARE PARTAKERS OF THE DIVINE NATURE.

Now, yes, you can find verses in the Bible where people speak of themselves this way. The Psalms contains numerous references to our depravity. Even Paul's epistles contain verses that could be taken to say that we are all helplessly and hopelessly broken, corrupt and sinful. But those verses are not the entire picture.

For example, when Paul talks about his wretched condition in the epistle to the Romans, he says:

"For I know that good itself does not dwell in me, that is, in my sinful nature. For I have the desire to do what is good, but I cannot carry it out. For I do not do the good I want to do, but the evil I do not want to do—this I keep on doing. Now if I do what I do not want to do, *it is no longer I who do it, but it is sin living in me that does it.*

"So I find this law at work: Although I want to do good, evil is right there with me. For in my inner being I delight in God's law; but I see another law at work in me, waging war against the law of my mind and making me a prisoner of the law of sin at work within me. *What a wretched man I am! Who will rescue me from this body that is subject to death?"* (Romans 7:18–24, emphasis mine)

A few things to notice here: First, that Paul contrasts himself from his sin nature. See verse 18 where he affirms: "good itself does not dwell…in my sinful nature." He has a new nature that is in Christ, as he affirms numerous times in other writings:

"You were taught…*to put off your old self*…[and] *to be made new in the attitude of your minds; and to put on the new self,* created to be like God in true righteousness and holiness." (Ephesians 4:22–24)

"since *you have taken off your old self* with its practices *and have put on the new self, which is being renewed in knowledge in the image of its Creator."* (Colossians 3:9–10, emphasis mine)

His new nature is, in some ways, at war with his old nature. But please notice that it is the sin nature that desires the wrong things. This is not Paul's current reality. He has been made new in Christ. This is why he ends this paragraph by saying, in verse 25:

"Thanks be to God, who delivers me through Jesus Christ our Lord!" (Romans 7:25)

The entire point he wants to make is that he has been set free from this tug-of-war.

It's amazing how much of our theology could be corrected if we just kept on reading the entire chapter of scripture, isn't it? This conclusion makes all the difference because it affirms that we are not helpless slaves to our sins. On the contrary. We are delivered and set free through the finished work of Christ.

This is also why if we keep on reading in the very next chapter that flows out of this one, Paul's statement:

> *"Therefore, there is now no condemnation for those who are in Christ Jesus, because through Christ Jesus the law of the Spirit who gives life has set you free from the law of sin and death.* For what the law was powerless to do because it was weakened by the flesh, God did by sending his own Son in the likeness of sinful flesh to be a sin offering. And so he condemned sin in the flesh, *in order that the righteous requirement of the law might be fully met in us, who do not live according to the flesh but according to the Spirit. Those who live according to the flesh have their minds set on what the flesh desires; but those who live in accordance with the Spirit have their minds set on what the Spirit desires."* (Romans 8:1–5, emphasis mine)

So, Paul's point here is not that we are powerless creatures who are slaves to our sinful natures. Far from it! His point is that we now have the power *"not [to] live according to the flesh but according to the Spirit."*

Because Christ took on flesh in solidarity with all humanity at His Incarnation and become one with us—even as He was One with the Father and the Spirit—we are all now co-crucified with Christ.

Because of this, we who were crucified with Him are now also raised with Him and seated with the Father in the Heavenly places. This is what Paul wants us to understand. The old has gone. The new has come.

We are not "sinners" any longer. We are children of God. We are new creatures made alive in Christ.

We are not worms. And, in fact, God never speaks of us this way. You will never find one verse where God says that we are worms, or garbage, or unworthy of His love, mercy or compassion.

We speak this way about ourselves, but God does not speak this way about us.

For example, here are a handful of verses in the New Testament where we hear God's heart for us expressed in terms of love. Pay close attention to these passages because I want to ask you something about them:

"For God so *loved* the world..." (John 3:16, emphasis mine)

"The *love* of God is higher, wider, longer and deeper than anyone can imagine" (Ephesians 3:14–21, emphasis mine)

"Nothing will ever separate us from the *love* of God" (Rom. 8:31–39, emphasis mine)

"*Love* is patient. *Love* is kind. *Love* keeps no record of wrongs." (1 Corinthians 13, emphasis mine)

"God is *love*. Whoever lives in love lives in God, and God in them." (1 John 4:7–21, emphasis mine)

Now, do you know what you will never read just after (or before) any of these verses about the extravagant love that God has for you? You will never once read anything about the wrath of God to "balance" out this teaching. You also never once read any statements about how you and I are unworthy of God's love, or how we can't earn or deserve God's love.

Instead, what we read is page after page, verse after verse of the fantastic, endless, transformative *love* of God that is poured out on us night and day like a never-ending waterfall.

So, like it or not, we are loved.

FEARING THE GOD OF LOVE?

What I don't understand is why some Christians are so eager to shut down this focus on the love of God. Why does it seem they are so afraid of a God whose character is defined by such radical love? Why are they threatened by a God who *is* love?

Perhaps an even better question is: Why are some Christians more afraid of a God of love than they are of a God of Wrath? That is something I legitimately do not comprehend.

WHY ARE SOME CHRISTIANS MORE AFRAID OF A GOD OF LOVE THAN THEY ARE OF A GOD OF WRATH?

Maybe this is closer to "Big Brother" syndrome? As when the prodigal son returns home and the Father forgives him so completely and quickly and throws the party for him, it's the older brother who can't handle it. He hates the idea of this extravagant love being shared with his brother—the "sinner"—who deserves to be put out with the servants.

In fact, in that story the only person who demands retribution is the older brother. Not the Father. It's the Father who ventures outside the house to explain to the elder son why mercy is better than judgment and why love is the best response. The older brother is the one with the wrath. The Father is the one who responds with love.

So, often, we are the ones who are crying out for vengeance, because as my friend Brad Jersak points out, *"We have to admit that our version of justice is mostly indistinguishable from revenge."*

Maybe the reason we are largely uncomfortable with God's mercy when it is extended to others is because we feel that "someone should have to pay for the evil that was done."

At one level, I can relate to that sentiment. But whenever people respond this way I often ask them, "So, are you saying that you really hope that God will punish you for all the bad things you did in this life after you die?"

Usually they just look at me and blink in momentary confusion. But then they say, "No, that's not what I mean. My sins are covered by the blood of Christ. I'm talking about those other people who have done really bad things."

And that's the point. We never think of our own sins as the sort that must be punished. We're totally ok with Christ forgiving us through the cross. But, it's those *other sinners* we really want to suffer in order for justice to be served.

So, what we're missing in this conversation is this: God has dealt with all of our sins. He has forgiven us all through Christ. We are all now reconciled to Him. The mercy we have received, and that we treasure and hold dear, is not only good for us, it's good for everyone.

Yet, justice must still be served. Not through retribution or punishment, as we have already seen. But through reconciliation and restoration. All of us have things in us we need to have healed. We have wounds that need to be tended to. God will not only heal us, He will heal the ones who hurt us, and then they will also receive healing for the scars that twisted them into the sorts of people who harmed us. The entire cycle of harm and the complete legacy of suffering will be made right again. God is committed to making all things new, and this includes everyone who has ever harmed us, and everyone we ourselves have harmed.

THE SEPARATION MYTH

One of the myths we embrace about God's response to our sinfulness is rooted in our belief that the Father and the Son were separated on the cross when the sins of the world were placed upon Jesus.

We've all heard those sermons about how this was the moment where the Trinity was—for the first time in eternity—forced to endure separation.

The thing is, there is not one single verse in the entire Bible that ever teaches anything remotely like this.

Yet, we've all heard this preached so many times from the pulpit that we have come to accept it as a fact. Even though the Gospels never teach this. Even though Paul never says this. Even though the idea that the Father and the Son experienced separation at the cross is never once mentioned anywhere in the entire Bible. We believe it.

So, where does this teaching come from? How did creep into our consciousness? Why do we believe it?

The teaching that the Father turned away from Jesus on the cross, and that Jesus experienced separation from the Father comes from a few assumptions. Let's look at two:

First, the assumption that God is too holy to look upon sin.

Second, the assumption that when Jesus said, "My God, my God! Why have you forsaken me?" (Matthew 27:46) from the cross that this was the moment when His Father actually did forsake him.

Let's take these two assumptions one at a time and see if they are true.

First: Is God really too holy to look upon sin? Not at all. We've covered this in great detail already. The two verses from the Old Testament used to teach this doctrine actually go on to affirm that God *does* look upon our sins. So, this is easily dismissed.

Second: When Jesus says, "My God, my God, why have you forsaken me?" doesn't that mean that His Father really did forsake Him?

No, it doesn't. Here's why. This statement from Jesus was the opening stanza from Psalm 22 which begins:

"My God, my God, why have you forsaken me? Why are you so far from saving me, so far from my cries of anguish?" (v. 1)

This is a Messianic Psalm where we read prophetic statements like:

"...they pierce my hands and my feet." (v. 16)

"...They divide my clothes among them and cast lots for my garment." (v. 18)

If anything, Jesus is quoting this Psalm from the cross because he hopes to point out how these exact words are being fulfilled at that very moment.

Now, let's note also what this same Psalm has to say about what God is doing while Jesus is on the cross:

"For he [God] has not despised or scorned the suffering of the afflicted one; *he has not hidden his face from him* but has listened to his cry for help." (v. 24, emphasis mine)

That's right. The Psalmist actually says that they will pierce the hands and the feet of the Messiah, and that they will divide his clothes and cast lots for his garments...and that God *"will not hide His face from him."*

So, is it true that the Father turned His face away from Jesus when He was on the cross? No. It is not true.

In fact, Jesus affirms that His Father would never abandon Him:

"Jesus replied. "A time is coming and in fact has come when you will be scattered, each to your own home. *You will leave me all alone. Yet I am not alone, for my Father is with me."* (John 16:31–33, emphasis mine)

Here Jesus not only affirms that His Father will not leave him—even though the disciples will—but also that this abandonment by the disciples and the ever-present nature of the Father occurs at the same time: While Jesus is hanging on the cross!

Now, this really should not surprise us. God promises all through the scriptures that He will never leave us or forsake us, and Jesus reminds us that He will be with us always, even unto the end of the age.

So, to recap: The Father did *not* look away from Jesus while He was on the cross.

Why does this matter? Because if the Father won't forsake Jesus when all of the sins of the world are laid upon him, then God will not forsake you either. No matter what you've done. You are not forsaken. You are not rejected.

WHY DOES THIS MATTER? BECAUSE IF THE FATHER WON'T FORSAKE JESUS WHEN ALL OF THE SINS OF THE WORLD ARE LAID UPON HIM, THEN GOD WILL NOT FORSAKE YOU EITHER. NO MATTER WHAT YOU'VE DONE. YOU ARE NOT FORSAKEN. YOU ARE NOT REJECTED.

ATTACK OF THE "LOVE BUTS"

There is no "God is Love...but" verse in the New Testament. There is only love. Endless, boundless, unending, unrelenting, exceptional, amazing, fantastic, glorious love that we can only experience to believe and receive.

We are *loved* by a God who *is* Love! We were created by this God of Love—in God's image—so this means we are *loved!* Created by Love, in the image of *love*, to *be* Loved.

This is who we are.

Love is who God is.

Love is what God does.

Loved is who we will always be.

Hopefully one day those who call themselves followers of Jesus will relax and get comfortable with the idea of a God who really is love, inside and out. No "ifs", "ands" or "buts" allowed.

Is that hard to accept? For some of us, yes. If so, maybe it's because we've grown up hearing this worm theology reinforced over and over again.

Is this hard for you to accept? If so, maybe there were some Christians in your church experience who poured shame over you.

Maybe there were pastors and teachers who preached messages of condemnation to keep you under control.

Maybe there were some worship leaders who planted melodies in your heart that emphasized your previous experience as a worm and a wretch.

But that's not who Jesus says you are. Not at all. In fact, my friend Dan Notti put together a very helpful list of who we are according to the New Testament. It's pretty impressive, I think.

Here's who we are:

We are sons and daughters.

"See what great love the Father has lavished on us, that we should be called children of God! And that is what we are!" (1 John 3:1)

We are filled with the fullness of Christ.

"And I pray that you, being rooted and established in love, may have power, together with all the Lord's holy people, to grasp how wide and long and high and deep is the love of Christ, and to know this love that surpasses knowledge—that you may be filled to the measure of all the fullness of God." (Ephesians 3:17–19)

"And God placed all things under his [Christ's] feet and appointed him to be head over everything for the church, which is his body, the fullness of him who fills everything in every way." (Ephesians 1:23)

We are new creatures with a new nature.

"Therefore, if anyone is in Christ, the new creation has come: The old has gone, the new is here!" (2 Corinthians 5:17)

"...since you have taken off your old self with its practices and have put on the new self, which is being renewed in knowledge in the image of its Creator." (Colossians 3:9-10)

We are holy and dearly loved

"Therefore, as God's chosen people, holy and dearly loved, clothe yourselves with compassion, kindness, humility, gentleness and patience." (Colossians 3:12)

"But you are a chosen people, a royal priesthood, a holy nation, God's special possession, that you may declare the praises of him who called you out of darkness into his wonderful light." (1 Peter 2:9)

The truth is, the New Testament is chock full of truth about our new identity in Christ, and it is all good.

Jesus affirms our worth.

"So don't be afraid; you are worth more than many sparrows." (Matthew 10:31)

Jesus declares our freedom.

"Then you will know the truth, and the truth will set you free... So if the Son sets you free, you will be free indeed." (John 8:32;36)

"It is for freedom that Christ has set us free." (Galatians 5:1)

Jesus calls us his friends, not slaves.

"I no longer call you servants, because a servant does not know his master's business. Instead, I have called you friends, for everything that I learned from my Father I have made known to you." (John 15:15)

Jesus says that He and the Father will come and make their home in us.

"Jesus replied, 'Anyone who loves me will obey my teaching. My Father will love them, and we will come to them and make our home with them.'" (John 14:23)

We are not condemned.

"Therefore, there is now no condemnation for those who are in Christ Jesus..." (Romans 8:1)

We are always loved.

"Who shall separate us from the love of Christ? Shall trouble or hardship or persecution or famine or nakedness or danger or sword?...For I am convinced that neither death nor life, neither angels nor demons, neither the present nor the future, nor any powers, neither height nor depth, nor anything else in all creation, will be able to separate us from the love of God that is in Christ Jesus our Lord." (Romans 8:35–39)

We are forever connected with God for eternity.

"God has said, 'Never will I leave you; never will I forsake you.'" (Hebrews 13:5)

If you ever forget who you are, please refer back to this amazing list of promises and remind yourself as often as possible.

FILTHY RAGS VS PREGNANT FAITH

Often, when I speak against the evils of "Worm Theology" someone will ask me what I think about the verse that says:

"For all of us have become like one who is unclean, And all our righteous deeds are like a filthy garment..." (Isaiah 66:6)

First of all, I need to point out what this verse is *not* saying: It is not saying that *we* are "filthy rags." What it says is that "all our *righteous deeds* are like a filthy garment." Big difference.

What it means is that my attempts to become righteous by my own works are equal to a "filthy garment", and that word in the Hebrew is literally the term for a "menstrual rag."

(Hold that thought for a moment and we'll come back to it, I promise).

So, very simply, this verse is telling us that our own efforts to achieve righteousness based on our own "good works" are equal to a menstrual rag.

God is not calling you or me or anyone else a "filthy rag" here. That's not what is being communicated.

Now, let's go back to the "menstrual rag" metaphor. Why use this image in reference to our own attempts at righteousness? Because a woman's period is when the unfertilized egg is expelled from the body in an issue of blood.

It's a mental picture of a failure to conceive new life within the womb. That's key to what we're about to see next.

In the New Covenant scriptures, Jesus says something astounding along these same lines:

"Now this is eternal life: that they know you, the only true God, and Jesus Christ, whom you have sent." (John 17:3)

This is a direct inversion of the Old Covenant scripture referenced above about "filthy rags." How? Because the word Jesus uses here for "know" is the Greek word *"Ginosko"* which is the term for sexual intercourse between a man and a woman.

Stay with me here.

The prophet Isaiah tells us in the Old Covenant that our attempts at righteousness are like a menstrual cloth: A failure to fertilize an egg and produce life.

Then Jesus tells us in the New Covenant that eternal life is when we have an intensely intimate connection with God which conceives new life within us.

So, our attempts to become righteous by our own efforts are like an unfertilized egg in the reproductive cycle which is flushed away by a menstrual period.

Actual life is only possible when we have such an intimate knowledge [*Ginosko*] and connection with God that it conceives new life within us.

So, that "filthy rags" image is not only *not* about us being filthy creatures in God's eyes, it's actually a much more profound picture of how we can only find real life and experience true transformation by drawing nearer to God in an intimate relationship of lover and beloved.

When we finally embrace our identity as God's beloved and fully immerse ourselves in an intimate connection with this Divine Love, we suddenly discover what we were always intended and designed to experience: Love unending and Life abundant.

EMBRACING THE TRUTH

The truth is, there is nothing—not one single thing—you and I need to do to be loved by God.

Why? Because we are already loved by God—totally, completely, unequivocally, and absolutely—with an everlasting love.

Our sin does not separate us from God's love. Our failures do not either.

Nothing will ever separate us from the Love of God. Not angels. Not demons. Not the future. Not the past. No height. No depth. Nothing in all of creation.

Why? Because God is love. This means that God's entire nature is to love. It is who God is.

And what about us? Who are we? We are created by God into the image of God. This means we are created by love into the image of love.

God, who is love created us in the image of love to be loved. This is who we are. We are loved. We are forever defined by this love. Nothing will ever change our identity as those who were created by love, in the image of love, to be loved. Not even death will change this. In fact, even if we are totally unaware of these realities, we are still loved.

So, we can be ignorant of this love. We can forget about it. We can even deny this is true. But none of that will actually mean that at any time we are not still loved by a God who is love and who created us in the image of eternal love. Like it or not—believe it or not—you are still loved with an everlasting love that will never die, never end, never go away, never fade, never cease, and never, ever stop.

Now, you may not feel it right now. In fact, you might feel like total garbage. You might feel like you can't go on. You may think that no one could ever really love you this way. You might even believe that you don't deserve such unimaginable love. *But you're wrong.*

- Your feelings are not true. Your belief about unworthiness is simply false.

- Even when you don't feel loved, you are still loved.

- Even when you don't feel worthy of this love, you are still loved.

- Even when you doubt it, you are still loved.

- Even when you feel like garbage. You are still loved more than you will ever know.

To be honest, I don't always feel loved either. Sometimes I feel like crap. Sometimes I forget these things are true about me, and about God. I start to drift into depression or doubt. I wrap myself in a shroud of sadness and wallow in my feelings of unworthiness.

Even though I know in my heart and mind that these feelings of being unloved by God are not true, I can still feel the pain sometimes. We all do.

> WHEN I QUIETLY STOP AND REMEMBER WHO GOD IS, AND WHO I AM, IT HELPS ME TO RECONNECT WITH REALITY—WITH THE ULTIMATE REALITY THAT GOD IS LOVE AND THAT I AM LOVED.

In those moments, what helps me is to stop and intentionally sit in silence. When I quietly stop and remember who God is, and who I am, it helps me to reconnect with reality—with the ultimate reality that God is love and that I am loved.

See, happiness is not something external to me. It's not an object "out there" somewhere that I need to find in order to reach contentment. Neither is joy, nor hope, nor peace. Those things are not outside of me. They are not things I need to acquire.

Why? Because ultimately what makes me happy is knowing that I am loved. Once I stop and meditate on the truth, I realize that love is who I am. I am loved by the One who is Love and I was created by Love to be an expression of this Love, along with everyone—and everything—else in the Universe.

So, my being loved is what leads to happiness, and peace, and joy. These are not things I do not possess. They are, in fact, things I am.[3]

Heaven, by definition, is the place where God dwells. So, if I dwell with God, I dwell in Heaven. So, where does God dwell? In me. As Jesus says, "My Father and I will come and make our home in you." (John 14:23) And as the author of 1 John says: "God is love, and those who live in love live in God and God in them."

Paul also affirms to idol-worshipping pagans in Athens: "God is the one in whom we all live, and move, and have our being." (Acts 17:28)

God is love. God is near. Nothing will ever change this. So, if anything needs to change, it's my perception of these things. I can accept it, or I can deny it. But either way, the truth remains: I am loved. And so are you.

Now, repeat after me: *"I am not a worm. I am a dearly loved child of God. Jesus lives and breathes in me right now. He will never leave me. He will never forsake me. His love for me will never die."*

Now, set your eyes on Jesus, the author and finisher of your faith. Place your hope in Him, the One who loves you beyond measure.

Start living every day, moment by moment, in the new reality of your identity in Christ. If you can, try helping others to see that they are not worms, either. We all need a lot more worm-free Christianity.

Need a reminder of how God really sees you? Once more I want to share another list of statements about your identity compiled by my friend Dan Notti because this is the truth about who you are:

I AM ACCEPTED

- I am God's child (John 1:12)

- I am Jesus's friend (John 15:15)

- I am justified. (Romans 5:1)

- I am united with Christ and one in Spirit with Him (1 Corinthians 6:17)

- I have been bought with the highest price and I belong to God forever (1 Corinthians 6:19–20)

- I am a member of His Body (1 Corinthians 12:27)

- I am His adopted child (Ephesians 1:5)

- I have direct access to God through the Holy Spirit (Ephesians 2:18)

- I have been redeemed and totally forgiven of every sin (Colossians 1:14)

- I have been established, anointed and sealed by God (2 Corinthians 1:21-22)

- I have been given God's glorious grace lavishly and without restriction (Ephesians 1:5,8)

- I am brought near to God through Christ's blood (Ephesians 2:13)

- I am included. (Ephesians 1:13)

- I have received the incomparable riches of God's grace (Ephesians 2:7)

- I am the focus of God's kindness (Ephesians 2:7)

- I am not condemned. (Romans 8:1–2)

- I am blameless (1 Corinthians 1:8)

- I am united with other believers in Christ (John 17:20–23)

I AM SECURE

- I am secure in Christ (Ephesians 2:20)

- I am not alone (Hebrews 13:5)

- I am free from any charges of condemnation against me (Romans 8:31)

- I cannot be separated from God's love (Romans 8:35)

- I have been established, anointed and sealed by God (2 Corinthians 1:21–22)

- I am hidden with Christ in God (Colossians 3:3)

- I am confident that the good work God started in me will be perfected (Philippians 1:6)

- I am a citizen of heaven (Philippians 3:20)

- I have not been given a spirit of fear (2 Timothy 1:7)

- I have been given power, love and a sound mind (2 Timothy 1:7)

- I can find grace and mercy in my time of need (Hebrews 4:16)

- I am born of God and the evil one cannot touch me (1 John 5:18)

- I am blessed with every spiritual blessing (Ephesians 1:3)

- I have hope (Ephesians 1:12)

- My heart and mind are protected by God's peace (Philippians 4:7)

- I am protected (John 10:28)

- I am victorious (1 Corinthians 15:57)

- I am overcoming (1 John 4:4)

- I am safe (1 John 5:18)

I AM A NEW CREATION

- I am born again (1 Peter 1:23)

- I am a new creation (2 Corinthians 5:17)

- I am complete in Christ (Colossians 2:10)

- I am holy and blameless (Ephesians 1:4)

- I am a saint (Ephesians 1:1)

- I belong to God (1 Corinthians 6:20)

- I am in Him (Ephesians 1:7; 1 Corinthians 1:30)

- I have been redeemed (Ephesians1:8)

- I am sealed with the promised Holy Spirit (Ephesians 1:13)

- I am raised up with Christ (Ephesians 2:6; Colossians 2:12)

- I am seated with Christ in heavenly realms (Ephesians 2:6)

- I am alive with Christ (Ephesians 2:5)

- I am qualified to share in His inheritance (Colossians 1:12)

- I have the mind of Christ (1 Corinthians 2:16)

- I am growing up into Christ (Ephesians 4:15)

- I am dead to sin (Romans 1:12)

- I can know God's will for my life (Ephesians 5:17; Romans 12)

- I am crucified with Christ (Galatians 2:20)

- I have eternal life in Christ (John 6:47)

- I have abundant life in Christ (John 10:10)

CHAPTER 6

GIRARD'S EPIPHANY

"...the persistent mistake of supposing that sin-offerings must some-how have been meant to propitiate God by the killing of a victim in the offerer's stead, [is] an idea which has been a source of endless confusion in the exegesis of the New Testament."

– O.C. QUICK[1]

One of the most insightful perspectives on the cross of Christ and the meaning of the crucifixion in the last twenty years has come from a seemingly unexpected source. Rene Girard, a professor of Language, Literature and Civilization at Stanford University, saw something so profound and mysterious—a truth about humanity, sin and sacrifice—that was hiding in plain sight all along. His perspective on the essence of human nature unlocks the mysteries of our need for redemption and reveals the fundamental core of our being that Jesus illuminates, heals and restores through the incarnation, crucifixion and resurrection.

To begin with, let's simply take a look at how human beings learn. We are wired from infancy to grow and develop language and communication skills, survival cues, and the adoption of cultural norms through a mechanism called "mimesis." Simply put, a baby born in Japan learns to speak Japanese by observing her parents, mimicking sounds and following the speech patterns she hears others speaking. All other infants learn their languages the same way. We also learn how to dress, how to behave, what is acceptable within our culture, how men and women relate to one another, what foods are good, what practices are acceptable, and on and on; all through the built-in process of mimesis.

So, on one level mimesis is a necessary development and survival mechanism that all human children rely on to become who they will eventually be as adults. But there's a dark side to mimesis as well. We observe this whenever we see a toddler in a room full of toys who ignores every other plaything except the one in their hand. Now, try introducing another toddler into the room and you will see the darker side of mimesis when the second child picks up a toy and begins to enjoy it. Suddenly, the first child forgets about the toy they were holding and tries to forcibly remove the one from the second child's hands, emphatically shouting, "Mine!"

THIS MIMETIC DESIRE IS ONE OF THE ROOTS— PERHAPS EVEN THE TAPROOT—OF NEGATIVE HUMAN BEHAVIOR OR SIN, AS WE HAVE COME TO KNOW IT.

And here we have the foundational tension within humanity. Girard refers to this as "Mimetic Desire" and argues that we as humans do not know how to develop desires of our own without first observing what others desire:

> "One always desires whatever belongs to that one, the neighbor. "Since the objects we should not desire and nevertheless do desire always belong to the neighbor, it is clearly the neighbor who renders them [the objects] desirable…We assume that desire is objective or subjective, but in reality it rests on a third party who gives value to the objects…our neighbor is the model for our desires. This is what I call mimetic desire."[2]

This mimetic desire is one of the roots—perhaps even the taproot—of negative human behavior or sin, as we have come to know it. The bulk of the Ten Commandments are centered around the same basic assumptions of this theory. Our desires are what lead us into violence, adultery, theft, conflict and war. So, the Ten Commandments focus on the fruit of our mimetic desires—*You shall not kill, You shall not commit adultery, You shall not steal, You shall not bear false witness against your neighbor*—and the final commandment summarizes our basic problem this way:

> "You shall not covet [Hebrew "chamad", meaning "desire"] the house of your neighbor. You shall not covet the wife of your neighbor, nor his male or female slave, nor is ox or ass, nor anything that belongs to him." (Exodus 20:17)

So, understanding our innate problem that is rooted in our mimetic desires is foundational. If we become aware of the fact that we all struggle with a built-in tendency to mimic the desires of others and try to understand how that leads us to desire the things that those around us have, then we can begin to understand what drives our tendency to engage in behaviors we have come to term sinful: violence, theft, adultery, etc.

The Old Testament Law sheds light on our misplaced desire and commands us not to sin against our neighbors in these ways. But it fails to give us any solutions to deal with the irresistible reflex we all are born with—the desire to have the things that others desire. The Law merely reveals the problem and encourages us to try as hard as we can to resist those desires if possible.

Ironically, even with this basic problem spelled out in the Ten Commandments, most of us are oblivious to this mechanism at work within us. This blind spot prevents us from becoming aware that we are participating in the increasingly mimetic rivalry that has infected everyone around us.

As Girard explains:

"Mimetic desire does not always result in conflict, but it frequently does so for reasons the tenth commandment makes evident. The object I desire in envious imitation of my neighbor is one he intends to keep for himself, to reserve for her own use; she will not let someone snatch it away without combat... but...nine times out of ten my desire will resist this and become even more intense in imitating the desire of its model.

"Opposition exasperates desire, especially when it comes from the man or woman who inspires the desire. If no opposition initially comes from him or her, it soon will, for if imitation of the neighbor's desire engenders rivalry, rivalry in turn engenders imitation. The appearance of a rival seems to validate the desire, the immense value of the object desired. Imitation becomes intensified at the heart of the hostility, but the rivals do all they can do to conceal from each other and from themselves the cause of this intensification. Unfortunately, concealment doesn't work. In imitating my rival's desire I give him the impression that he has good reasons to desire what he desires, to possess what he possesses, and so the intensity of his desire keeps increasing."[3]

So, once mimetic desire begins to take shape in our hearts it begins to grow—not only within us but within the heart of the one whose desires we are mimicking. We desire the object because they desire it. The more they see us desiring the object they desire, that desire grows even stronger because they can see that our desire for it is even stronger than their own. The rivalry grows and escalates until something breaks that power or resolves that conflict. Quite often, if the object of the desire is something that cannot be purchased or acquired in some other way, the resolution of the desire may be expressed in some form of violence or theft. Until a resolution comes, the desire begins to grow, and eventually to fester and rot within us. Desire for the object turns to hatred for the other person. That can quickly turn to something darker if we're not careful to find our way out of this mimetic rivalry.

On a larger scale, this basic human tendency towards mimetic desire becomes the foundational basis for mankind's conflict and suffering over the centuries. Once we expand the principle of mimetic desire expressed between two people outward to include the mimetic desires of communities, or nations, we can see where things grow exponentially violent and ugly.

ON A LARGER SCALE, THIS BASIC HUMAN TENDENCY TOWARDS MIMETIC DESIRE BECOMES THE FOUNDATIONAL BASIS FOR MANKIND'S CONFLICT AND SUFFERING OVER THE CENTURIES.

Girard explains it this way:

"*The mimetic nature of desire accounts for the fragility of human relations.* Our social sciences should give due consideration to a phenomenon that must be considered normal, but they persist in seeing conflict as something accidental, and consequently so unforeseeable that researchers cannot and must not take it into account in their study of culture. *Not only are we blind to the mimetic rivalries in our world, but each time that we celebrate the power of our desire we glorify it...*When we are devoted to adoring our neighbor, this adoration can easily turn to hatred because we seek desperately to adore ourselves, and we fall... *the principal source of violence between human beings is mimetic rivalry, the rivalry resulting from imitation of a model who becomes a rival, or of a rival who becomes a model.*" (emphasis mine)[4]

So, our blindness to this mechanism at work within us, and within all of humanity, is what allows the process to continue. We participate in this dance of mimetic rivalry and suffer the consequences of it, but we are helpless to understand how we were caught up into these feelings and behaviors. Girard's theory explains the core of our problem and shows us how the Scriptures illuminate the source of our struggle and conflict.

Again, he explains:

"*Such conflicts are not accidental, but neither are they the fruit of an instinct of aggression or an aggressive drive.* Mimetic rivalries can become so intense that the rivals denigrate each other, steal each other's possessions, seduce the other's spouse, and, finally, they even go so far as murder. I have just mentioned again, though this time in reverse order, the four major acts of violence prohibited by the four commandments that precede the tenth...*If the Decalogue devotes its final commandment to prohibiting desire for whatever belongs to the neighbor, it is because it lucidly recognizes in that desire the key to the violence prohibited in the four commandments that precede it.* If we ceased to desire the goods of our neighbor, we would never commit murder or adultery or theft or false witness. *If we respected the tenth commandment [against wrong desires], the four commandments that precede it would be superfluous.*" (emphasis mine)[5]

So, most human conflicts, then—jealousy, rage, theft, murder, war, genocide—originate from our inability to escape this mimetic rivalry that begins with mimetic desire at the individual level. Yet, we are oblivious to our participation in this process. We fail to see it in ourselves, or in others. And so, the power of this mimetic rivalry and desire continues to hold sway over each and every one of us.

JESUS DOESN'T ASK US TO TRY TO STOP MIMICKING THE DESIRES OF OTHERS. INSTEAD, JESUS INVITES US TO IMITATE HIM; TO FOLLOW HIM; THE ONE PERSON WHO DOES NOT PARTICIPATE IN THE SORT OF MIMETIC RIVALRY OF OTHERS.

As we also mentioned above, the Ten Commandments attempt to make us aware of this process, but offers us no hope of escaping it, only the admonition to stop doing something that we are helpless to stop doing.

This is where Jesus comes in. He seems to understand our human weakness to mimic the desires of others and to pattern ourselves after our neighbors, leading to conflict, rivalry, division and violence. So, his solution is an elegant one. Jesus doesn't ask us to try to stop mimicking the desires of others. Instead, Jesus invites us to imitate him; to follow him; the one person who does not participate in the sort of mimetic rivalry of others.

This conscious imitation, unlike the unconscious [or subconscious] mimicry, is an intentional decision to follow the example of Christ in our daily life. As Matthew Distefano explains: "Creative or positive mimesis needs to be conscious, whereas negative mimesis is 'below phenomenological awareness.', according to psychologists like Dr. Scott Garrels."[6]

The difference with Jesus is that he does not desire what those around him desire. Not at all. Instead, Jesus only desires to do what the Father is doing. This changes everything.

Now, rather than simply being told to stop desiring our neighbor's wife, ox, house, property, we are now shown *how* to do this: By desiring what we see Jesus desiring, which is to do the will of the Father as He says: *"I only do what I see the Father doing."* (See John 5:19)

So, if we understand that to break the Ten Commandments is defined as "sin", then this is how Jesus "saves us from our sins"— by showing us how to obey those commandments—and sets us free from the power of our sins which lead to death.

As we follow Jesus; as His desires become our desires; we finally discover our way out of this seemingly inescapable spiral of mimetic desire and rivalry. As we abide in Christ and Christ abides in us, our hearts become transformed from the inside out. We no longer desire to have the things our neighbors have. Instead, we freely share all that we have with those among us who are in need, as we see those first Christians doing in Acts once they are filled with the Holy Spirit. This is the evidence that the power of mimetic desire and rivalry are finally broken, when people suddenly begin to spontaneously sell their property in order to provide food for those who have none, or simply by sharing what they have with others.

This is what it looks like when people are set free from the insidious power of mimesis:

> "All the believers were together and had everything in common. They sold property and possessions to give to anyone who had need. Every day they continued to meet together in the temple courts. They broke bread in their homes and ate together with glad and sincere hearts, praising God and enjoying the favor of all the people." (Acts 2: 44–47)

This subversion and inversion of mimesis comes when we follow Jesus and mimic His heart's desire to do what He sees the Father doing, which is expressed by blessing everyone and extending mercy, grace and love to all.

Jesus offers us a model of mimesis that is not based on desiring what others have, but based on love which creates within us a holy desire to bless our neighbors with good things rather than a desire to take their things away for ourselves.

Girard puts it this way:

> "*What Jesus invites us to imitate is his own desire, the spirit that directs him toward the goal on which his intention is fixed: to resemble God the Father as much as possible*…His goal is to become the perfect image of God. Therefore he commits all his powers to imitating his Father. *In inviting us to imitate him, he invites us to imitate his own imitation*…Jesus, by contrast, invites us to do what he himself does, to become like him a perfect imitator of God the Father…Why does Jesus regard the Father and himself as the best model for all humans? Because neither the Father nor the Son desires greedily, egotistically. God 'makes the sun rise on the just and the unjust.' God gives to us without counting, without marking the least difference between us…If we imitate the detached generosity of God, then the trap of mimetic rivalries will never close over us." (emphasis mine)[7]

Another way that we can experience the negative aspects of mimesis is when we give in to the crowd. In spite of how much we may believe we are immune to this mimetic power, the truth is that when we are in the minority it is much too easy to become swayed by the crowd. This is why Jesus, when confronted by the Pharisees with the woman caught in adultery, challenges the men standing there to consider first their own sinfulness and then asks the one who is sinless to "cast the first stone." Why is this first stone the most difficult to throw? Because, as Girard points out, "…it is the only one without a model."[8]

This is what happens to Peter when he denies Jesus three times. His stated intention prior to this was to die along with Jesus, even if everyone else were to abandon him, surely Peter would never do this. However, only a few short hours later as Peter stands alone among those in the courtyard who are not passionate disciples of Jesus, he finds himself being swayed to the crowd. This is why he pretends not to know Jesus and eventually curses emphatically to deny any connection to Jesus. Why? Not because there was some special flaw in Peter that the rest of us don't have. On the contrary, Peter is just like all of us. When we are alone in the crowd we go along with the crowd. We smile at the party when people start insulting our friend who isn't there. We pretend not to see someone we care about when we're in the company of another group of people we hope to impress. We keep silent when others mock someone who is gay, even though our best friend, or our child is gay. We fold like a house of cards as soon as we are threatened with alienation from the crowd. This is mimesis. We all do it. And the only way out of this trap is to follow Jesus; to do what we see the Father doing; to speak up for the outcast; to show mercy to the wounded and the offender; to suffer the shame heaped upon them both if necessary in order to shine a light on the power of mimesis.

This is an example of something Girard says is rooted in the scapegoat mechanism, and we need to understand what it is in order to fully appreciate what Jesus was doing on the cross.

Here's how it works: Two people, or two nations, both desire the same thing: an object, a person, or a vital resource like water or fertile farmland. The thing desired is immaterial. The rivalry exists and it threatens to erupt into conflict which may eventually, inevitably turn violent and perhaps even deadly for one side or the other. In this situation, one of two things will happen: One will do violence to the other until only one remains to claim the object of the desire. Another possibility, however, is that the tension between these two parties could be resolved by the destruction of a shared enemy or a scapegoat.

We all know the phrase, *"The enemy of my enemy is my friend,"* but perhaps a more Girardian phrasing might be *"The enemy of my rival is my friend."* At any rate, the principal is the same. The two parties involved in mimetic conflict realize that they both share a hatred for another and by destroying that person (or persons) they resolve the violent tensions between themselves and enjoy a season of peace.

This process is so cathartic that the people perceive it as a Divine revelation or gift. They may often begin to see the scapegoat as Divine in origin since, to them, it is the only way to explain the miraculous way it saved both sides from extinction and brought peace, seemingly, out of thin air.

We see examples of this in the Gospels, for example, when it tells us that Herod and Pilate were enemies prior to their encounters with Jesus, but after both of them examined Jesus, tortured him and eventually ended up putting Jesus to death, it says this:

> "Then Herod and his soldiers ridiculed and mocked him. Dressing him in an elegant robe, they sent him back to Pilate.

That day Herod and Pilate became friends—before this they had been enemies." (Luke 23:11–12, emphasis mine)

So, what was it that brought Herod and Pilate to a place of peace and friendship? It was their shared disdain and ridicule of Jesus that brought them together.

What does this have to do with why Peter gave in to the crowd and denied Jesus? Everything. Because it is the mimetic power of the crowd that overcomes Peter's desire to stand with Jesus to the very end. He intends to champion Jesus, but when the time comes he is powerless to overcome the mimetic force that bends his will to the crowd.

See, Peter instinctively understood that the crowd's intention was to make Jesus the scapegoat. Nothing was going to change that. Once he stood staring into the gaping jaws of certain death at the hands of the mob, he realized it was just too easy to go along with the crowd and avoid the same fate. And that's the point: It's easier to go along with this process than it is to fight against it. In fact, to fight against the scapegoating mechanism once it is in motion—as it was in the case of Jesus after his arrest in the Garden—requires such an inhuman amount of strength, it was practically inevitable that Peter would do exactly as he did—and as we all have done at one time or another—when faced with this irresistible mimetic power of the crowd. He surrendered to the will of the people.

This is even what Pilate does when faced with the angry crowd that demands to have Jesus cruci-fied. He says over and over that he does not find any fault in Jesus. He implores the people to accept

AND THIS IS THE POINT: EVEN SOMEONE LIKE PILATE WHO HOLDS THE AUTHORITY OF THE ROMAN EMPIRE AT HIS COMMAND CANNOT RESIST THE MIMETIC POWER OF THE CROWD ONCE THEY HAVE FOUND THEIR SCAPEGOAT.

another scapegoat—Barrabas, who was a convicted criminal—but they will not be dissuaded. And this is the point: even someone like Pilate who holds the authority of the Roman Empire at his command cannot resist the mimetic power of the crowd once they have found their scapegoat. Pilate's only option is to wash his hands and allow the process to play itself out.

The scapegoat mechanism isn't even very well hidden in the Gospels, and frankly that is part of the power of them. We see Caiaphas the High Priest explain the process quite openly when he says of Jesus:

> "You do not realize that it is better for you that one man die for the people than that the whole nation perish." (John 11:50)

See, he understood that the existing tension between the Jewish people and the Roman Empire at the time had reached a critical point. He knew that either an armed rebellion was about to break out between the two sides, or that a common scapegoat had to be killed in order to bring a temporary truce between the two nations. Jesus was that scapegoat. And for about 40 years it did bring a form of peace between the Roman Empire and the occupied Jewish people. However, we must be very careful not to accuse the Jewish people of some special form of evil, as if we would not have done what they did. Girard warns us that:

> "The anti-Semitic interpretation fails to discern the real intention of the Gospels. It is clearly mimetic contagion that explains the hatred of the masses for exceptional persons, such as Jesus and all the prophets; it is not a matter of ethnic or religious identity. The Gospels suggest that a mimetic process of rejection exists in all communities and not only among the Jews."[9]

So, Jesus is inevitably crucified to satiate the mimetic demands of the people for a scapegoat. This brings an end to the tension. Peace is restored, but only for a short period of time. Eventually the mimetic tension will begin to build again and then another scapegoat must be found or violence will spill over and one side will be destroyed.

Girard explains this way:

"This spontaneous lynching is what reestablishes peace and, with the victim as intermediary, gives this peace a religious, a divine, meaning. Once the victim is killed, the crisis is over, peace is regained, the plague is healed, all the elements become calm again, chaos withdraws, what is blocked or locked or paralyzed is opened, the incomplete is completed, gaps are filled, and the confusion of difference is restored to proper differentiation."[10]

Both Peter and Paul are finally converted to Christ when they have eyes to see their ignorant participation in this mimetic violence. Peter had to endure the shame of his denial and realize that there was a power at work in him that he had been unaware of until that moment. Paul had to come face-to-face with Christ on the road to Damascus to discover that he had been persecuting Jesus as he went from house to house arresting Christians and putting them to death.

Again, Girard summarizes this beautifully when he says:

"Because of the simple fact that we live in a world whose structure is based on mimetic processes and victim mechanisms, from which we all profit without knowing it, we are all accessories to the Crucifixion and persecutors of Christ. The Resurrection empowers Peter and Paul, as well as all believers after them, to discover that all imprisonment in sacred violence is violence done to Christ. Humankind is never the victim of God; God is always the victim of humankind."[11]

So, now that we understand how mimetic desires rule our hearts and turn us into people who desire what belongs to others; and how this process leads us to conflict and violence, we can now also see how Jesus came to set us free from all of that. He showed us the only way to break out of mimetic desires that lead to violence by redirecting our desires to mimic His own desires; which is to want what the Father wants and to do what we see the Father doing. This leads us to desire blessings for our neighbors and empowers us to "love our neighbors as ourselves," which in turn allows us to become more like Jesus in all that we do, breaking once and for all the power of mimetic rivalry and desire. In this way, Jesus has truly "saved us from our sins."

JESUS WENT THE EXTRA MILE TO SURRENDER TO OUR MIMETIC VIOLENCE, TO SUFFER UNDER OUR COLLECTIVE DENIAL OF HIM AND TO DEMONSTRATE THAT THE POWERS THAT HAVE RULED HUMANITY HAVE ALWAYS BEEN FOUNDED ON THIS SAME VIOLENCE.

Jesus went the extra mile to surrender to our mimetic violence, to suffer under our collective denial of him and to demonstrate that the powers that have ruled humanity have always been founded on this same violence.

> "His suffering on the cross is the price Jesus is willing to pay in order to offer humanity this true representation of human origins that holds it prisoner. In offering himself in this way," Girard says, "he deprives the victim mechanism of its power in the long run...the powers are not put on display because they are defeated, but they are defeated because they are put on display."[12]

In other words, by submitting to this process, Jesus exposes this scapegoating mechanism and our mimetic violence for what it really is. In the cross we see who we really are and we see who God really is.

The cross is where God declares that He will never use His power and authority against us. Even though God has all the power in the universe, at the cross He makes is clear that He will never use that power to harm us or manipulate us in any way. In fact, Jesus not only lets go of His power in the Incarnation, taking on the form of a servant, He goes so far as to say to us,

"Here, I'll give you complete power over me. Do whatever you want to me. Beat me. Whip me. Mock me. Torture me. Nail me to a cross. I will still love you. I will always forgive you. Now, will you trust me?"

At the cross Jesus shows us the heart of a Father God who would rather die than live without us; who submits to our violence and suffers under our wrath and still finds enough love within to proclaim His complete forgiveness for us because He knows we "know not what [we] do."

> AT THE CROSS JESUS SHOWS US THE HEART OF A FATHER GOD WHO WOULD RATHER DIE THAN LIVE WITHOUT US; WHO SUBMITS TO OUR VIOLENCE AND SUFFERS UNDER OUR WRATH AND STILL FINDS ENOUGH LOVE WITHIN TO PROCLAIM HIS COMPLETE FORGIVENESS FOR US BECAUSE HE KNOWS WE "KNOW NOT WHAT [WE] DO."

Once we understand Girard's concept of mimesis and how it shapes human behavior, and even our own unconscious desires, the scandal of the cross comes into focus for us. We can begin to see why Jesus was crucified, what was going on in the hearts and minds of everyone around him at the time, and how the cross shines a light on the entire mimetic process of scapegoating we all participate in without knowing it.

Now the cross takes on a profoundly new meaning for us. It becomes the focal point where mankind's sinfulness is on full display and God's power to heal us is revealed at last. Once the veil is removed and we have eyes to see the inner workings of our mimetic desires we understand what it is we are saved from. We see in Jesus our only hope of salvation from this way of living. Our desire becomes redirected towards Jesus so that we can—like Him—truly desire to do what we see the Father doing as He extends mercy, compassion and love to everyone regardless of their social standing, religious affiliation or ethnic background.

This is the true power of the cross. First, it shows us who we are, then it reveals to us who God is, and finally it empowers us to experience a transformation of the heart that fundamentally changes us from the inside out.

The cross is not where God killed His son so He could forgive us. The cross is where we killed God's son and God's forgiveness set us free. By exposing our sins and showing us how to break free of our mimetic desires, Jesus has opened the door of salvation to all of humanity. We just need to walk this path and learn to abide in Christ daily to experience our own personal resurrection.

CHAPTER 7

WHY DOES JESUS SAY THAT HE DIED?

"Sacrifice is not, in the first place, an activity of human beings directed to God and, in the second place, something that reaches its goal in the response of divine acceptance and bestowal of divine blessing on the cultic community. Rather, sacrifice in the New Testament understanding—and thus in its Christian understanding—is, in the first place, the self-offering of the Father in the gift of his Son, and in the second place the unique response of the Son in his humanity to the Father, and in the third place, the self-offering of believers in union with Christ by which they share in his covenant relationship with the Father."

— EDWARD J. KILMARTIN[1]

As we rethink the cross and question the theological assumptions of Penal Substitutionary Atonement, the question "Why did Jesus have to die?" begins to come into sharper focus for us. We can see how our sins did not truly separate us from God and how this separation was only in our minds, as Paul says:

> "Once you were alienated from God and were enemies *in your minds* because of your evil behavior. But now he has reconciled you by Christ's physical body through death to present you

holy in his sight, without blemish and free from accusation…"
(Colossians 1:21–22, emphasis mine)

Our realization is that, now, through Christ, we are all reconciled to God—and this reconciliation is on our side, not on
God's side. God was always wanting us to come to Him, but we
were the ones who believed that our sins made that impossible.
Jesus shows us that we are forgiven by freely forgiving everyone
he meets—even those unbelieving pagan soldiers who were in
the process of nailing him to the cross.

We learn that God was, in Christ *not* counting our sins against
us, but reconciling us to Himself. (See 2 Corinthians 5:19)

We learn that "God is love" (1 John 4:8) and that "love keeps
no record of wrongs" (1 Corinthians 13:5), so we are "loved with
an everlasting love" (Jeremiah 31:3) which "transcends knowledge" (Ephesians 3:19) and "nothing in all creation will ever be
able to separate us from the love of God that is in Christ Jesus…
[not] death nor life, neither angels nor demons, neither the present nor the future, nor any powers, neither height nor depth,
nor anything else…" (Romans 8:38–39) and this love is "higher,
wider, longer and deeper" than anything we can comprehend
(Ephesians 3:18).

Even so, we still haven't taken the time to listen to Jesus when
it comes to answering the question: "Why did Jesus die?"

This is part of our problem. We almost exclusively draw from
the writings of the Apostle Paul to find answers to these questions about the crucifixion—not that there's anything wrong
with that, per se—but if we fail to go to Jesus—the one who was
actually crucified—for reasons why he died, we have failed in
our quest for answers.

My friend Bruxy Cavey was the first person to help me
identify this blind spot in our conversations about atonement

theology. As he sees it, there are 4 specific reasons that Jesus gives us for why he died and what he accomplished for us through the crucifixion:

> "Starting with his own words, [Jesus identifies] these four reasons for his death. Those would be Healing, Freedom, Unity and to establish the New Covenant."²

To unpack those four reasons, let's take some time to examine each one in turn:

HEALING

Just before John 3:16, Jesus reminds the Pharisee Nicodemus of the serpent that was lifted up in the wilderness by Moses. (See John 3:14-15) In the Old Testament story being referenced, the Children of Israel were sick. They were dying and their healing came when they looked up in faith to a bronze serpent that Moses had been commanded by God to fashion. All anyone had to do in that case was to look up and see the serpent that Moses had lifted up and when they did they were all healed of what was killing them. This is a metaphor that Jesus uses to tell us that—somehow—his death on the cross will become an instrument of our healing. In this metaphor, we might say that our sins are what has poisoned us and that Jesus surrenders to crucifixion as a way of healing us from the fruit of that sin.

FREEDOM

In Mark 10:45 Jesus says, "For even the Son of Man did not come to be served, but to serve, *and to give his life as a ransom for many.*" (emphasis mine)

In this verse, we see that another metaphor is used to show us that—somehow—the death of Jesus secures our freedom from the bondage of sin and death.

As Bruxy Cavey puts it: "In other words Jesus says, "I'm going to do whatever it takes to get you free. That's not just about sin, that's also anything else that holds us down and keeps us in bondage; that's the ways of religion, legalism, addiction to that authoritarian top-down coercive power...I'm going to heal you from what's killing you and I'm going to free you up from what's oppressing you."[3]

UNITY

In John 12:32 Jesus says, "...when I am lifted up I will draw all people myself." The word translated as "draw" in the Greek literally means "to drag", so Jesus is saying that once he is "lifted up" on the cross, he will "drag" all people to Himself. This is a picture of reconciliation, attraction, and unity between Christ and all of us.

What Jesus tells us is that his death on the cross will woo our hearts and draw us near. Perhaps it is the humility of Jesus that touches people. Maybe it's the way he forgave those who were nailing him to the cross? Maybe it's the way he remembered his mother in that moment of excruciating agony and asked his disciple, John, to care for her? Or maybe it's simply the fact that Jesus was an innocent man who was tortured and executed for a crime he did not commit? Whatever it may be, I think that the cross most certainly draws people to Jesus. Even non-Christians often admit that they find Jesus fascinating and compelling. This is partially what is meant by "dragging all people" to Himself. Perhaps what is also meant by this is how his death declared everyone forgiven and reconciled to God.

But, drawing all mankind to Himself is not merely about bringing people to Jesus, or even about revealing God's true heart to us—although it most certainly accomplishes both of these things—but it is also about creating unity between individuals.

Jesus prayed that we "would be one as [He] and the Father are one" (John 17:11) and that in our oneness with Christ and the Father, we would also be one with one another.

> "My prayer is…that all of them may be one, Father, just as you are in me, and I am in you. May they be in us so that the World may believe that you have sent me. I have given them the glory that you gave me, that they may be one as we are one." (John 17:20–22)

The point, then, is for all of us—all of humanity—to be one with Christ and the Father (through the power of the Holy Spirit) and that unity with God makes all of us one with one another, in the same way the Spirit, the Son and the Father are One.

As astounding as this truth may be, it may be even more astounding when we begin to understand the implications of this oneness with God and with one another.

Baxter Kruger masterfully unpacks this concept for us here:

> "And thus what we discover and begin to believe is that in Jesus we too are with and in his Father in the Holy Spirit. But even here we must go further, or we rob Jesus and his gospel of his unearthly assurance and joy. For the us that faith discovers to be in Jesus Christ, with and in his Father and Holy Spirit, is the us as we are, in all our brokenness and sin and shame. Faith believes in this shocking, unearned Triune embrace, which Jesus made real and abiding within our darkness and unbelief, our apostasy and treachery. As such, this faith begets hope and the freedom to know and be known, to be loved and to love."[4]

Our being drawn into this mystical union of God and Humanity is not something any of us need to earn or deserve.

We simply experience it because it has already been accomplished through the finished work of Christ. This also means that our fellow humans are not required to earn this gift—as if any gift could be "earned"—but they, like all of us, have simply become recipients of these same great riches made possible by the power of the Incarnation, Crucifixion, Resurrection and outpouring of the Spirit on all flesh.

THE NEW COVENANT

Finally, we see where Jesus declares in the upper room that his death is the inauguration of the New Covenant between God and mankind.

> "In the same way, after the supper he took the cup, saying, "This cup is *the new covenant in my blood, which is poured out for you.*" (Luke 22:17–20, emphasis mine)

Jesus boldly declares that the New Covenant between God and all mankind is inaugurated by his death on the cross. What this means is that God is now in direct communication and connection with all humanity. As we read in Hebrews 10:16, the New Covenant (quoting from Jeremiah 31:31) says:

JESUS BOLDLY DECLARES THAT THE NEW COVENANT BETWEEN GOD AND ALL MANKIND IS INAUGURATED BY HIS DEATH ON THE CROSS. WHAT THIS MEANS IS THAT GOD IS NOW IN DIRECT COMMUNICATION AND CONNECTION WITH ALL HUMANITY.

"This is the covenant I will make with them after that time, says the Lord. I will put my laws in their hearts, and I will write them on their minds." Then he adds: "Their sins and lawless acts I will remember no more."

So, now under this New Covenant, everyone is forgiven, everyone has a new heart, everyone is welcomed, everyone is loved, everyone participates, everyone receives the Holy Spirit, everyone is welcomed into the Holy Priesthood of God, everyone becomes the Temple of the Holy Spirit, everyone becomes the daily, living sacrifice of God, and everyone has a one-to-one, direct connection to God because His Spirit has been poured out on all flesh and both Jesus and the Father have now come to make their home is every one of us.

How have we missed this? Perhaps because, as Bruxy reminds us, "Jesus's own voice has been underrepresented in Atonement Theology. Instead, we've gone straight to Paul. Not that Paul teaches anything different, but Paul plays backup singer to Jesus's solo career."[6]

So, unless we start with Jesus first, we'll miss the foundation of what Paul is building on. For example, 2 Corinthians 5:17 where Paul says:

> "Therefore, if anyone is in Christ, the new creation has come:
> The old has gone, the new is here!"

This is Paul expounding on how Christ has set us free and made us one together with Himself. Later on in the same chapter Paul says:

> "God made him who had no sin to be sin for us, so that in him we might become the righteousness of God." (2 Corinthians 5:21)

This is Paul agreeing with Jesus that his death brought us healing from sin and set us free to live a new kind of life. Paul also affirms that the death of Christ established the New Covenant. (1 Corinthians 11:25)

The problem, then, becomes our filter. If we begin with Jesus, then our filter will help us to see the scriptures through the lens of Christ. But if we begin with Calvin, or Augustine, or Luther, or Anselm, or even Paul, then our view will be filtered through those assumptions.

As Bruxy observes:

"Once you buy into Penal Substitutionary Atonement as your operative theory you filter everything through that. So, then, Protestant Theologians tend to rethink the Ransom idea as a payment to free us from God's wrath. But Jesus doesn't say any of that. He only says that he died to give us freedom."[6]

So, if we start with Jesus and listen to what he says about why he died and what it accomplished, we'll see that it was all about setting us free, healing what kills us, drawing us all to Himself, and to one another, and establishing a New Covenant where all things are made new and we participate in what God is doing in the world through our Divine connection with God and Christ through His Holy Spirit.

Perhaps now that we have come this far, we should take some time to reflect on everything we've learned about the atonement, the cross, forgiveness, sin, and salvation to see what it all means for us today.

That's what we'll cover in our next chapter.

CHAPTER 8

SUMMARY AND CONCLUSION: WHAT DOES IT ALL MEAN?

"Christ has no body now but yours. No hands, no feet on earth but yours. Yours are the eyes through which he looks compassion on this world. Yours are the feet with which he walks to do good. Yours are the hands through which he blesses all the world. Yours are the hands, yours are the feet, yours are the eyes, you are his body. Christ has no body now on earth but yours."

— TERESA OF AVILA

"[St Augustine was] a towering genius whose inability to read Greek and consequent reliance on defective Latin translations turned out to be the most tragically consequential case of linguistic incompetence in Christian history."

— DAVID BENTLEY HART

As we have seen, the topic of the crucifixion is quite complicated. The easy answers we were given in Sunday School and heard from the pulpit may have tried to simplify the cross for us, but at the same time these simplifications often obscured the deeper meaning of the event and may even have kept us from fully understanding what was—and what was not—happening on the cross when Jesus was crucified.

Here's what we've learned so far:

ATONEMENT THEORIES ARE NOT THE GOSPEL

Atonement Theories were developed over many hundreds of years—often in response to the theory which came before it—as a way of making sense of the cross. In each of these, we see not only the struggle of the Christian Church to fully explain the crucifixion, but we also notice that there was no real consensus of thought regarding this doctrine. Some emphasized God's love, others emphasized Christ's example, and still others focused more on God's justice and holiness.

ATONEMENT THEORIES ARE BASED ON METAPHORS. AS WITH ALL METAPHORS IT'S ALWAYS WISE NOT TO PUSH THEM TOO FAR.

Church Historian and Theologian J.F. Bethune-Baker summarizes it this way:

"Of the various aspects of the Atonement which are represented in the pages of the New Testament, the early Fathers [Pre-Reformation] chiefly dwell on those of sacrifice (and obedience), reconciliation, illumination by knowledge, and ransom… There is no suggestion of any satisfaction of the divine justice through the sufferings of Christ… *It is at least clear that the sufferings of Christ were not regarded as an exchange or substitution of penalty, or as punishment inflicted on him by the Father for our sins. There is, that is to say, no idea of vicarious satisfaction, either in the sense that our sins are imputed to Christ and his obedience to us, or in the sense that God was angry with him for our sakes and inflicted on him punishment due to us.*" (emphasis mine)[1]

THE DANGER OF OVERANALYZING ATONEMENT METAPHORS

Atonement theories are based on metaphors. As with all metaphors it's always wise not to push them too far. The dangers of doing so can obscure the original simplicity and create new problems for us to solve, as Bruxy Cavey warns us:

> "As predominantly Greek-inspired Gentiles flooded into this Jewish movement with their philosophical assumptions, we began to overanalyze the metaphors which were offered to make one simple point and make us see the beauty of it. The point of the ransom is freedom. But early theologians…[began] over-analyzing the beauty of the metaphor which merely wants us to understand that Jesus will do whatever it takes to set us free."[2]

The same could be said of every single one of these various atonement theories that men have developed over the centuries. An honest desire to make sense of the cross has been expressed in different ways over time, and these metaphorical pictures of Christ's death have each emphasized one aspect of the crucifixion that is worthy of examination. However, the more we become distracted by the minutiae of these metaphors, the easier it is to miss the point. We focus on the individual trees and miss the entire forest.

THE ERRORS OF PENAL SUBSTITUTION

In this book, our main focus is to expose the folly of the Penal Substitutionary Atonement theory developed by John Calvin. Not only has this theory dominated Western Christian Theology over the last several hundred years, it has done great damage to our proper understanding of God's true heart and character as revealed to us through Jesus Christ.

As we've seen, the main ideas promoted by PSA theory are as follows:

- God is too Holy to look upon our sins

- God's Holiness and our sinfulness creates separation from God

- God's primary response to our sins is to punish

- God's wrath must be satisfied

- Jesus suffered under the Father's wrath

- God's wrath is now satisfied, and forgiveness is now possible

We have already gone through each of these points so far and demonstrated that they are not supported by the scriptures.

God is *not* too Holy to look upon our sins. There are no verses in the Bible that suggest this is true, and in fact, there are numerous verses that contradict this notion.

God's Holiness and our sinfulness does *not* separate us from God. The only separation between God and mankind is what we perceive in our minds. God's desire has always been reconciliation, not separation.

God's primary response is *not* punishment. Rather, God's response to our sins is always mercy, grace, love and forgiveness. Jesus forgave everyone. He never waited for confession or repentance. He simply forgave. Jesus said he only did what he saw the Father doing. So, if Jesus's response to our sins was always forgiveness, it's because this is how the Father responds to our sins.

God's wrath is *not* expressed on the cross. Instead, what we see is that the wrath of mankind was poured out on Christ. We murdered Jesus. God's response was to raise him from the dead.

As Paul reminds us, "God was, in Christ, not counting our sins against us but reconciling the world to Himself." (2 Corinthians 5:19)

The term "Wrath of God" in the New Testament is Paul's reference to the Law which brought sin and death and is presented in contrast to the Law of Christ which brings us life, hope, forgiveness and mercy. Even where the term "Wrath of God" seems to refer to an outpouring of God's judgment upon us, the reality is that this experience is simply the result of reaping what we have sown. God does not cause the judgment but rather does all He can to warn us so that we may avoid it. The same way a loving parent would warn a child not to touch a hot stove, God always pleads with us to change our behavior so that we can reap the fruit of love and compassion rather than suffer under the pain of our own selfishness, pride and violence.

So, it is not true that God so hated the world that He sent His son to take the bullet of His wrath on the cross. God does not require a sinless virgin child sacrifice to forgive us. God is not Zeus or Baal or the volcano god whose wrath must be satisfied with human blood. This is not who God is. Nor is it the God revealed to us by Christ.

> GOD DOES NOT REQUIRE A SINLESS VIRGIN CHILD SACRIFICE TO FORGIVE US. GOD IS NOT ZEUS OR BAAL OR THE VOLCANO GOD WHOSE WRATH MUST BE SATISFIED WITH HUMAN BLOOD. THIS IS NOT WHO GOD IS.

What's more, even if PSA theory were true it would still not be the Gospel. We know this because the Gospel that Jesus preached is clearly spelled out for us in the Gospels of Matthew, Mark and Luke, especially. It is the "Good News" of the Kingdom of God which Jesus proclaimed, and the Apostles preached and Paul also affirmed specifically on 8 different occasions in the New Testament.

What is the Good News of the Kingdom? It is the announcement that we can all enter into the very presence of God right now.

God's Kingdom is here. It is alive within us right now. We do not need to wait until after we are dead to experience this amazing reality. Jesus is "Emmanuel"—God with us—and He has promised never to leave us or to forsake us.

WORM-FREE CHRISTIANITY

We are not worms. We are not wretches. We are not worthless scum. We are the beloved children of God. We have been made in the image of God—who is love—and so we are also infused with God's love from the very beginning.

Penal Substitution twists the Gospel to say:

- Jesus saved us from the Father (not our sins)

- God's wrath put Jesus on the cross (not our wrath)

- For God so hated the world….(not "For God so loved the world")

- God requires a virgin child sacrifice to forgive us

All of these are false. Not one of those things is affirmed by Jesus, or the Apostles or the New Testament, or the early Christians prior to the Reformation in the 16th Century.

When we look at the New Testament what we actually see is something much more glorious and beautiful:

- God is love (1 John. 4:8;16)

- All who live in love live in God and God in them (1 John 4:16)

- God is *not* too Holy to look upon our sins (Jeremiah 16:17; Heb. 4:13)

- God responds to our sin with forgiveness (2 Corinthians 5:19; Hebrews 8:12)

GOD DOES *NOT* REQUIRE BLOOD SACRIFICE TO FORGIVE US

As we've already seen, this is a false assumption based on a misunderstanding of a verse in Hebrews which reads, "without the shedding of blood there is no forgiveness of sins" (Hebrews 9:22). This is a statement of what was required *"under the Law"* and is only mentioned in contrast to the "better covenant" we have through Christ; a covenant that is not about bloodshed or sacrifice but about simple, humble obedience to God's desire that we love one another as Christ has loved us.

> "How and why would God need a 'blood sacrifice' before God could love what God had created? Is God that needy, unfree, unloving, rule-bound, and unable to forgive? Once you say it, you see it creates a nonsensical theological notion that is very hard to defend."[3]

The truth of scripture is that God forgives all the time without bloodshed—in both the Old and the New Testament—and the idea of sacrifice was not God's idea, but ours.

UNDER THE PSA MODEL, JESUS COMES TO SAVE US FROM HIS OWN FATHER'S WRATH. BUT THIS IS NOT WHAT THE SCRIPTURES SAY. WE'RE TOLD THAT JESUS CAME TO SAVE US FROM OUR SINS, NOT FROM GOD.

JESUS SAVES US FROM OUR SINS (NOT FROM GOD)

Under the PSA model, Jesus comes to save us from His own Father's wrath. But this is not what the scriptures say. We're told that Jesus came to save us from our sins, not from God. (See Matthew 1:21)

As we've seen, one of the ways that Jesus "saves us from our sins" is to show us a model to follow that is not selfish, or based on mimetic conflict but on *"doing what we see the Father doing"* which is to love our neighbor and desire what's best for them.

As Richard Rohr shows us:

"[This] view grounds Christianity in love and freedom from the very beginning. It creates a coherent and positive spirituality, which draws us toward lives of inner depth, prayer, reconciliation, healing, and universal at-one-ment, instead of any notion of sacrifice, which implies God needs to be bought off.

"Nothing changed on Calvary, but everything was revealed as God's suffering love—so that we could change!

"Jesus was precisely the "once and for all" (Hebrews 7:27) sacrifice given to reveal the lie and absurdity of all "sacrificial" religion. But we perpetuated such regressive and sacrificial patterns by making God the Father into the Chief Sacrificer, and Jesus into the necessary victim. Is that really the only reason to love Jesus? Is there no wondrous life to imitate?

"This "being saved by his death" language allowed us to ignore Jesus' way of life and preaching, because all we really needed Jesus for was the last three days or three hours of his life. This is no exaggeration. The irony is that Jesus undoes, undercuts, and defeats the sacrificial game. Stop counting, measuring, earning, judging, and punishing—ways many Christians are very well trained in—because they believe that is the way God operates too. This makes the abundant world of grace largely inaccessible—which is, of course, the whole point.

"It is and has always been about love from the very beginning."[4]

The widespread popularity of Calvin's Penal Substitutionary Atonement Theory is especially curious when you consider how little evidence can be found for it in the Scriptures. As noted Biblical Scholar and author David Bentley Hart points out:

> "*[PSA] is absolutely absent from the New Testament.* There's a sort of way to read it into the text because 16th century translators wrote it in, in a sense, by how they chose to translate certain words. *But there is seriously no good New Testament scholar who really understands the culture and the languages of the time and of the text who for a moment believes that this theology is to be found in Paul or in the Gospels or any of the other writings of the New Testament…In the New Testament and in the early Church, this is not how people thought about salvation, and it's certainly not what the Bible says about salvation.*" (emphasis mine)[5]

GOD'S WRATH IS OUR PROJECTION

We perceive God's wrath as punishment, but that's not reality. As the Psalmist has shown us:

> "With the merciful you show yourself merciful; with the blameless you show yourself blameless; with the purified you show yourself pure; and with the crooked you make yourself seem tortuous." (Psalm 18:25–27)

GOD NEVER WANTED SACRIFICES

Primitive cultures worshipped their gods through this sacrificial system where one person or animal had to shed blood before the god could come near and bless the people. The earliest followers of Yahweh in the Old Testament assumed their god was like all these other gods who demanded sacrifices. But over time, the God of the Old Testament clarified the fact that sacrifices were not required.

Rather than bloodshed, what God wants most from us is a relationship. God wants us to realize that it's about "*mercy, not sacrifice*" (Matthew 9:13) and this is expressed in the ways we love God and love others.

As Brad Jersak clarifies for us:

"*The meaning Christ attributes to sacrifice is simply this: laying one's life down for someone else* (John 15:13; 1 John 3:16). Anyone who gives their life to rescue another—whether it's a fireman dying while pulling someone from a flaming building; a policeman who's fatally wounded while rescuing a hostage; or a martyr stoned to death for preaching the good news—is 'paying the ultimate price.' Here, the metaphors are off the table. Here, sacrifice (laying down your life) is raw actuality—the events as they really happened. *Notice that this type of sacrifice has nothing to do with punishment, payment, retribution or appeasement. In every case, a life is given for the sake of the other, not to satisfy someone's wrath or placate their anger, but as a life-giving, life-saving sacrifice.*" (emphasis mine)[6]

GOD'S FORGIVENESS WAS NEVER ABOUT BLOODSHED

All through the scriptures we see God appealing to us to turn to Him, change our hearts, and seek His face. Forgiveness is always extended without the requirement for blood to be spilled.

> IN CHRIST, WE SEE
> EVEN MORE CLEARLY
> THAT FORGIVENESS IS
> OFFERED FREELY AND
> WITHOUT QUALIFICATION.

In Christ, we see even more clearly that forgiveness is offered freely and without qualification.

The type of sacrifice Jesus offered that God found pleasing and acceptable was in the expression of ultimate humility. This we see when Jesus takes on the form of a servant and lays aside immortality to put on mortal flesh.

As Jesus risks it all to demonstrate the Father's extravagant love for all humanity, he submits himself to our wrath and endures our violent judgment—even death on a cross.

This is why the author of Hebrews contrasts the "shedding of blood" requirement of the Law with the "better covenant" expressed in the humility of Christ. Even as we're told that God did not desire sacrifice, Jesus says that he "came to do [God's] will" which was not about sacrifice. Instead, Jesus adds "…but a body you have prepared for me…" and the author of Hebrews goes on to explain how Christ taking on flesh—in the incarnation—is how "we have been sanctified through the offering of the body of Jesus Christ once for all." (Hebrews 10:4–10) Not in the death of Christ, but through His life in the flesh which was a sacrifice of another kind.

In the primitive sacrificial model, the angry god's wrath is appeased through the offering of an innocent victim. But, in Christ, we see a loving God who submits Himself to *our* wrath and becomes the offering we have made of Him.

Christ also subverts the sacrificial model by reframing the New Covenant over a meal between friends; symbolized in the sharing of bread and wine around a table.

The death of Christ began at the Incarnation. When Jesus put on mortal flesh his death became inevitable. This is how the concept of sacrifice is redefined for us. When Christ becomes one with humanity, he agrees to experience everything we have experienced, including the experience of death.

The death of Christ, then, would have resulted in the salvation and transformation of all mankind, with or without the cross. Because the plan all along was for Christ to become incarnate in a body of flesh so that the seed of immortality could be planted into the soil of mortality. The resurrection power of Christ liberates us all from the power of the grave.

As Jesus phrased it:

"Truly, truly, I say to you, unless a grain of wheat falls into the earth and dies, it remains alone; but if it dies, it bears much fruit." (John 12:24)

So, it was always the plan for Christ to die. This is how the power of death was broken. The resurrection life of Christ invaded the realm of death and turned it inside out. The light of the world descended into the depths of outer darkness and illuminated it from within.

Or, as Paul phrases it in the inverse here in 1 Corinthians 15:

"For this perishable must put on the imperishable, and this mortal must put on immortality. But when this perishable will have put on the imperishable, and this mortal will have put on immortality, then will come about the saying that is written, "Death is swallowed up in victory. O death, where is your victory? O death, where is your sting?" The sting of death is sin, and the power of sin is the law; but thanks be to God, who gives us the victory through our Lord Jesus Christ." (1 Corinthians 15:53–57)

Because Christ the imperishable one took on perishable flesh, and because the immortal one became mortal, we [the mortal ones] are qualified to take on immortality—now that we are all "in Christ" and Christ is now in us.

So, in many ways, *how* Jesus died is irrelevant. Christ became flesh and experienced death so that we could put on immortality and share in the life of Christ forever. Paul says as much in the very same chapter of 1 Corinthians:

"But now Christ has been raised from the dead, the first fruits of those who are asleep. For since by a man came death, by a man also came the resurrection of the dead. For as in Adam all die, so also in Christ all will be made alive." (1 Corinthians 15:20–22)

Christ knew he would die from the start. But *how* he would die was not specifically relevant. Yes, his death was inevitable and even contingent upon the success of his mission. Once Christ took on mortal flesh everything was set in motion.

To be clear, God did not send Jesus *to be* crucified. We (humans) decided that Jesus would die in this way. But there was nothing magical or specific about crucifixion itself that accomplished God's plan. Christ's obedience, even unto death on a cross, is what mattered most.

What we did was kill Jesus. What God did was to raise him up again. We crucified Jesus. God did not.

Now, certainly, Jesus knew that he would most likely be crucified by the Roman authorities. That wasn't hard to guess. Even Plato predicted, hundreds of years prior to Christ, that a truly righteous man would be beaten and crucified if we ever got our hands on him.[7]

So, while the death of Christ was inevitable, his crucifixion was not.

The answer to the question, "Why did Jesus have to die?" is answered simply: "Because he became human at his Incarnation." But the answer to the question, "Why did Jesus die on the cross?" is answered by admitting that our reaction to Christ's innocence, righteousness and radical love was to nail him to that cross.

Yes, we can affirm that Christ died "because of our sins" in that it was our sin that nailed him to the cross. As Rene Girard has said,

> "…we live in a world whose structure is based on mimetic processes and victim mechanisms, from which we all profit without knowing it, [and because of this] we are all accessories to the Crucifixion and persecutors of Christ."[8]

But, even as we were in the process of nailing him there, his forgiveness was instantaneous and complete as he said, "Father, forgive them, for they know not what they do." (Luke 23:34)

CHRIST FULFILLED THE LAW

One thing Jesus made clear from the very beginning of his ministry was the purpose and scope of his mission:

> "Do not think that I have come to abolish the Law or the Prophets; I have not come to abolish them but to fulfill them." (Matthew 5:17)

JESUS CRACKS THE CODE WHEN HE TELLS US TO FOLLOW HIM—TO IMITATE HIS IMITATION OF THE FATHER—BECAUSE ONCE WE DESIRE TO DO WHAT THE FATHER IS DOING, WE ARE EMPOWERED TO LOVE OUR NEIGHBOR AS WE LOVE OURSELVES.

Jesus fulfilled the Law by showing us how to keep it. Whereas the Law only told us to stop desiring, it did not show us how to stop. Jesus cracks the code when he tells us to follow him—to imitate his imitation of the Father—because once we desire to do what the Father is doing, we are empowered to love our neighbor as we love ourselves.

Now, our desires are not to take away from our neighbors but to share every good thing we have with them because we love them as we are loved.

Now that we have disproven the theory of Penal Substitutionary Atonement, how do we understand and embrace the implications of what Christ has accomplished for us? That's what we'll cover in our final chapter.

CHAPTER 9

RADICAL TRANSFORMATION

"The cross does not provide salvation within a retributive justice framework. It provides salvation from a retributive justice framework."

— ALAN SMITH

"The cross of Christ is the place where humanity did everything we could to get God to stop loving us, and we failed miserably."

— BRUXY CAVEY

God, through Christ, has not only fulfilled the Law and the Prophets, overcome the power of death, shown us how to love others as we have been loved, broken the power of mimetic rivalry, redefined sacrifice, taken away our sins and made all things new, He has also made us one with Himself, and with one another.

> "For since death came through a man, the resurrection of the dead comes also through a man. *For as in Adam all die, so in Christ all will be made alive.*" (1 Corinthians 15:21–22, emphasis mine)

"But the gift is not like the trespass. *For if the many died by the trespass of the one man, how much more did God's grace and the gift that came by the grace of the one man, Jesus Christ, overflow to the many!* Nor can the gift of God be compared with the result of one man's sin: The judgment followed one sin and brought condemnation, but the gift followed many trespasses and brought justification. *For if, by the trespass of the one man, death reigned through that one man, how much more will those who receive God's abundant provision of grace and of the gift of righteousness reign in life through the one man, Jesus Christ!*

"Consequently, *just as one trespass resulted in condemnation for all people, so also one righteous act resulted in justification and life for all people.*" (Romans 5:15–18, emphasis mine)

THROUGH THE INCARNATION, CHRIST HAS BECOME ONE WITH ALL HUMANITY. THIS UNION OF GOD AND MAN THROUGH CHRIST ALLOWS FOR THE ENTIRE WORLD TO BE RESCUED FROM THE POWER OF SIN AND SET FREE FROM THE POWER OF DEATH.

Through the Incarnation, Christ has become one with all humanity. This union of God and man through Christ allows for the entire world to be rescued from the power of sin and set free from the power of death. Not only that, but this mystical union of flesh and spirit; God and Man; opens up incredible possibilities for all creation to be made new and transformed from the inside out.

As Jesus urges us to realize, "…I am in my Father, and you are in me, and I am in you." (John 14:20) This means the Incarnation is a declaration of God's eternal union with mankind. Jesus is in the Father. We are in Christ and Christ (who is in the Father) is in us. This speaks of a mind-bending paradox that defies the imagination, and yet we are told to realize that it is the truth. This is reality. We are in Christ and Christ is in us.

So, what happens to Jesus happens to us. What is true of Christ is true of us because of this miracle of Incarnation. We are in an eternal, unbreakable union with Almighty God through our abiding connection with Christ.

As C. Baxter Kruger so beautifully explains:

"As Jesus bowed to be slaughtered as an innocent lamb by the human race, he brought his oneness with his Father and the Holy Spirit—and his divine but jeopardized union with the human race—into the abyss of the great delusion where Satan has his hold. In so doing Jesus Christ the Creator meets us at our twisted worst, using our bitter rejection of him to bind us in union with him forever. Thus, the incarnate, crucified, and resurrected Creator Son secured his union with us by way of our unbelief, once and for all obliterating the threat of our nonexistence, rendering separation from him an eternal impossibility..."[1]

Our union with God in Christ through the Holy Spirit also affirms our union with all humanity: We are all one in Christ Jesus our Lord.

It is impossible for us as individuals to enjoy eternal oneness and union with God through Christ without also recognizing that all humanity is also intertwined in this same exact union and oneness with God through Christ.

So, everyone you meet, everyone you've ever know, everyone who has ever lived in the past or will live in the future is also one with Christ in the same way that you are one with Christ. We are all in Christ who is in the Father and they are in us—all of us.

Therefore, there is truly no such thing as "them" anymore. There is now only one eternal "us" that finds itself forever in union with God through Christ.

IT IS IMPOSSIBLE FOR US AS INDIVIDUALS TO ENJOY ETERNAL ONENESS AND UNION WITH GOD THROUGH CHRIST WITHOUT ALSO RECOGNIZING THAT ALL HUMANITY IS ALSO INTERTWINED IN THIS SAME EXACT UNION AND ONENESS WITH GOD THROUGH CHRIST.

"The Son is the image of the invisible God, the firstborn over all creation. For in him all things were created: things in heaven and on earth, visible and invisible, whether thrones or powers or rulers or authorities; all things have been created through him and for him. *He is before all things, and in him all things hold together.*" (Colossians 1:15–17)

The implications of this radical union we enjoy with God and one another through the miracle of the Incarnation is astounding and breathtaking. Just imagine, if the fall of Adam—a mere created being—could mire all humanity in sin for eons, what marvelous and miraculous realities are now unleashed upon mankind through the Incarnation of God in human flesh? If the Creator died, then we all died. If Christ resurrected, then so did we. If Immanuel ascended and now sits at the right hand of Almighty God, then so do we. Why? Because in Christ all Humanity was forever united with the Father for all eternity and now nothing can ever separate us.

CHRIST IN YOU

This amazing realization of Christ's Incarnation brings a deeper and more profound understanding to what the death of Christ and the resurrection of Christ really means.

God was in Christ when we nailed him to the cross. God was in Christ when he forgave us of our sins. God was in Christ when he descended into the depths of the grave. God was in Christ when he plundered the realm of the dead and led those in captivity to victorious new life. God was in Christ when Jesus rose from the dead. Because of this, all of humanity is set free from the power of sin and death.

But even more than this, God and Christ are in you. God and Christ are in union with all creation. This means everything is inside of God, and God is inside of everything.

Theologian David Bentley Hart explains it this way:

"There is nowhere we can go to escape God. Whether in "heaven" or in "hell" or any location or state of consciousness we can conceptualize. There is no "separation". Ever. No reality can exist in and of itself, or be self-sustained or void of God's presence. To find one's self within the realm of being is to find one's self in the mystery of God, the actualizer and energizer of being. For out of and through and into him are all things. All things. Which includes all things.

"God is not only the ultimate reality that the intellect and the will seek but is also the primordial reality with which all of us are always engaged in every moment of existence and consciousness, apart from which we have no experience of anything whatsoever. Or, to borrow the language of Augustine, God is not only 'superior summon meo'—beyond my utmost heights—but also 'interior intimo meo'—more inward to me than my inmost depths."[2]

Most of us have little trouble imaging that we are in Christ, or that Christ is in the Father. But the notion that everyone is in Christ, and therefore everyone is also in the Father, is another matter. We tend to think that it is only Christians who are "in Christ" but there are several scriptures that challenge this assumption.

For example, the Apostle Paul affirmed that everyone is in Christ and that God is the Father of all when he spoke to the idol-worshipping pagans in Athens and told them:

> WE TEND TO THINK THAT IT IS ONLY CHRISTIANS WHO ARE "IN CHRIST" BUT THERE ARE SEVERAL SCRIPTURES THAT CHALLENGE THIS ASSUMPTION.

"God is our father...and *the one in whom we all live and move and have our being.*" (Acts 17:28, emphasis mine)

But there are other verses that also affirm the idea that we are all in God/Christ and that God/Christ is in all of us. Such as:

> "And God placed all things under his [Christ's] feet and appointed him to be head over everything for the church, which is his body, *the fullness of him who fills everything in every way.*" (Ephesians 1:22–23, emphasis mine)

Now, if we follow the logic here we'll see what Paul is asserting. First, that God placed all things under Christ's feet and that the church is the body of Christ. No problem there. But then he goes a bit further to suggest that Christ "fills everything in every way" and that we—the Church—are filled with "the fullness of [Christ]."

So, if Christ is the head of the Church, and if we are His Body, and if Christ is the one who "fills everything in every way" and we are "filled with the fullness of Christ", then this is yet another way of affirming the very same idea that God is in Christ, and Christ is in the Father, and we are in Christ—all of us—and this union of God and Humanity is wider and deeper than we can imagine.

Here's another verse where Paul says:

> "Here there is no Gentile or Jew, circumcised or uncircumcised, barbarian, Scythian, slave or free, but *Christ is all, and is in all.*" (Colossians 3:11, emphasis mine)

Some believe that this verse is only applied to Christians, and this is the audience Paul is addressing in the passage, but the scope of the statement extends far beyond the limitations of a small group of people. The claim is that "Christ is all" and that Christ "is in all."

Now, it would be quite perplexing to claim that "Christ is all and is in all" if what you meant was that Christ was "in some" and "not all." As it would be logically inconsistent to argue that Christ is "the one who fills everything in every way" when what you intended to communicate was that Christ was "the one who fills some things in certain ways."

The language Paul uses in these passages affirms the idea that Christ really is "in all" and that Christ really is "the one who fills everything in every way" and that Christ really is "the one in whom we all live and move and have our being"—even idol-worshipping pagans who do not know the first thing about Jesus or the cross.

As we have seen "God is love and all who live in love live in God and God in them." (1 John 4:16)

The scope of God's union with us is infinitely greater than we have imagined. And this unity of Christ with humanity—and therefore humanity with Christ—extends beyond the individual person to encompass all of humanity with one another.

> THE SCOPE OF GOD'S UNION WITH US IS INFINITELY GREATER THAN WE HAVE IMAGINED. AND THIS UNITY OF CHRIST WITH HUMANITY—AND THEREFORE HUMANITY WITH CHRIST—EXTENDS BEYOND THE INDIVIDUAL PERSON TO ENCOMPASS ALL OF HUMANITY WITH ONE ANOTHER.

For example, if Christ is in everyone and if everyone is in Christ, then everyone is united together with one another through Christ.

This is the point where some of us draw the line. We still see ourselves as individuals and while we can accept the notion that we are one with Christ, and one with the Father through Christ, it's quite another thing to recognize that this union we share with Christ is also what connects us to everyone else.

But how could it be otherwise? How could any of us enjoy total union with Christ and still remain separated from each other? What sort of "unity" would that be? As Paul asks the Corinthian Christians: *"Is Christ divided?"* (1 Corinthians 1:13) and his reminder to all of us simply this:

"I appeal to you, brothers, by the name of our Lord Jesus Christ, that all of you agree, and that there be no divisions among you, but that you be united in the same mind and the same judgment." (1 Corinthians 1:10)

His point is that we are one in Christ and that in Christ there is no division. But we can act as if there is a division when we separate ourselves from each other. This is not only a denial of our actual unity in Christ, it goes against God's will for us which is that we "would be one even as [Christ] and the Father are one." (John 17:11)

This unity extends beyond merely our behavior towards one another. Certainly, the posture we take towards others is important, but it is not the final expression of our unity in Christ. It's *because* we understand that we *really are* one in Christ that we are driven us to express this unity outwardly. We do not pretend to have union because God asks us to. We have unity because we realize that *we are all already one in Christ.*

Once we embrace the profound truth of our unity in Christ, and how Christ makes us one with the Father who is in Him and in all of us, we can perhaps begin to allow these ideas to transform us from the inside out. The *metanoia* required—the ability to think differently about ourselves, and about God and the universe itself—is essential to our transformation from death into life; from darkness into the light.

"So from now on we regard no one from a worldly point of view. Though we once regarded Christ in this way, we do so no longer. Therefore, if anyone is in Christ, the new creation has come: The old has gone, the new is here!" (2 Corinthians 5:16–17)

What is necessary—we quickly realize—is a complete resurrection of our entire way of thinking and being and living. We absolutely must "repent" [metanoia]—think differently—about all we thought we knew of God, and of Christ, and even ourselves if we ever hope to comprehend just how completely the fabric of all humanity and creation has been forever changed by the Incarnation, Crucifixion and Resurrection of Jesus.

This is about more than being saved. It's about more than being forgiven. It's about so much more than going to heaven when we die. So much more.

Through the obedience of Christ and his Divine humility, all of creation has been incarnated in Him, crucified with Him, raised to newness of life with—and in—Him, and now this resurrection power is what permeates the entire universe. This is what holds all things together. There is nothing made that has not been touched by the presence of Christ. All things were created by Him and through Him and for Him. Everything is held perpetually in and through the One in whom we all live and move and have our being.

THIS IS ABOUT MORE THAN BEING SAVED. IT'S ABOUT MORE THAN BEING FORGIVEN. IT'S ABOUT SO MUCH MORE THAN GOING TO HEAVEN WHEN WE DIE. SO MUCH MORE.

Christ is the fullness of Him who fills everything and everyone in every way. We, through Him, are forever in union with the Father through the Spirit. Nothing will ever separate us from God or His Love. We now find ourselves floating in an endless ocean of God's presence because Jesus and the Father have come to make their home in us. (John 14:23) Their promise to us is that they will never leave us nor forsake us. (See Hebrews 13:5)

This is the beauty of the cross. This is the power of the resurrection. This is the miracle of the incarnation.

We are not objects of wrath. We are God's beloved children. We are not worms. We are made in the image of God. We are not covered in our sins. We have been washed clean forever. We are not sinners. We are forgiven. We are not in the hands of an angry God. We are in glorious union with the God who is love.

The more we embrace the vision God has for us—and for all humanity—the more we will begin to experience the transcending and transformative truth we were always intended to experience.

Let our focus be on how marvelous God is. Let us meditate on the "great love the Father has lavished upon us that we should be called the children of God—because that is who we are!" (1 John 3:1)

Let us dwell on this love that surpasses knowledge and that is infinitely higher and wider and longer and deeper than we can possibly imagine so that we "may be filled to the measure of all the fullness of God." (Ephesians 3:16–19)

Let us draw nearer to Christ so that we can learn how to emulate his imitation of the Father's heart to love everyone and show mercy to all because this is how we show that we "are Holy even as the Father is Holy." (Matthew 5:48)

Let us always remember that Jesus is in the Father and the Father is in Him, and He is in us, and we are in Him.

This is who we are. We are infused with Christ. Christ is infused with us. The Father is one with Christ, and with all of us at once. This makes us one with God and with one another in ways we have barely begun to comprehend.

If Christ was crucified before the foundation of the world, then what does that mean for us now? It means we were never separated from God. It means that we were in Christ before we were ever born. It means Christ was in us, and in everyone else who has ever lived, all along.

Behold, the Lamb of God who takes away the sins of the world is alive in you. You are now, and always have been, fully free and forgiven by God. You are now, and always have been, fully loved and treasured by God.

Nothing will ever change this reality. Nothing will ever separate you from God, or His great love for you.

Understanding who you are, and learning to live out of this breathtaking reality, is what you and I were made for. Take all the time you need to embrace your identity in Christ. The more you accept the fact that you are in Christ, and Christ is in you, and that you are loved with an everlasting love that nothing in the Universe can ever change, the more you will begin to transform into the person you were created to be.

My prayer for you is that you will come to accept—fully and completely and without a hint of wavering doubt—that you and Christ are inseparable and forever intertwined by the invincible power of Divine love.

You are immersed—at this very moment—in an ocean of love that is higher, wider, longer and deeper than you could possibly comprehend. Take all the time you need to explore those depths and navigate this space. It might even take an eternity to be honest. So just take your time. There's no hurry. But, once you get started, you may find yourself breathlessly eager to experience as much of this love as you possibly can.

The important thing to remember as you embark on this journey is this: You are not alone. Everyone and everything around you is infused with this same enduring presence of God's Spirit. This Love permeates every atom, every molecule and every space in between. You are connected to everyone else in ways you have yet to fully understand. But learning to see things with new eyes is also part of your transformation process. And don't lose heart, my friends, if you fail now and again along this path, because the good work that has already begun in you is something that God has promised to carry on to completion.

Behold, the old is gone and the new has come—and is coming—no matter what anyone else may say or do. The yeast is rising. The seed is growing. The vine is giving life to every branch.

The hope of glory is Christ in you. Hold on to this. He is holding on to you. And He will never let you go.

ADDITIONAL QUOTES ABOUT PENAL SUBSTITUTIONARY ATONEMENT THEORY

N.T. WRIGHT

"When Paul says that Jesus died for our sins, he adds the phrase 'according to the scriptures.' (1 Cor. 15:3) Now that doesn't mean, 'I can find three proof texts.' What it means is *there is an entire scriptural narrative which is about the Creator God who is rescuing the world and that scriptural narrative is shaped by the Exodus in particular, and by all the things that follow from the exodus. But then, coming through the whole story of Israel in exile where the people who are supposed to be bearing the solution for the world are themselves suffering the result of the problem. The Messiah, Israel's Messiah, comes to the point where that story has reached rock bottom in order to takes its weight upon Himself and so to begin a New Creation. There's Creation, Covenant, Exile and Restoration.*"

"*The clearest passage from Paul about this is Romans 8:3-4 when having just said 'there is no condemnation for those who are in Messiah Jesus', because the law of the spirit of life in Messiah Jesus has set you free from the law of sin and death, because God has done what the law couldn't do, since it was weak through the flesh, sending His own Son in the likeness of sinful flesh as a sin offering, He condemned sin in the flesh. There is no condemnation for us because God passed sentence of condemnation on sin—interestingly Paul doesn't say God condemned Jesus. He says God condemned sin in the flesh of Jesus. Here's one way of looking at it, which is from a reading of Romans 7 and 8, that God gave the Law in order to draw sin into one place, to lure sin into the place where it could be condemned; namely to Israel's representative [Jesus]. So, Jesus dies as the representative substitute, taking the condemnation on Himself, so having condemned sin, sin is now itself condemned and New Creation can begin. That's the energy of the Spirit taken forward."* (emphasis mine)[1]

BRAD JERSAK

"The essence of my point on substitution is this: Yes, there is a nuanced use of substitution that says, "Christ did for us what we could not do for ourselves. He stepped into the ring with Satan, sin and death in our stead."

"And yes, there is a nuanced use of penal that says, "What is the penalty or wages of sin? Death. Did Jesus die? Yes." So if Christ's death is [sort of] a substitution and he partakes in our death [the penalty of sin], is his death not a "penal substitution"?

"Some scholars like to use these nuances to retain the language of "penal substitution" (why?), pretending that the phrase itself can be dissected and read without regard for the historical intent (Calvinism) and its contemporary dominant use (Evangelicalism). And while careful experts such as Fleming Rutledge and NT Wright utterly reject any sense of wrath-appeasement in their atonement theology, they seem hesitant to reject the language of penal substitution (probably for ecumenical reasons). But wrath-appeasement is precisely what "penal substitution" means to all but an elite stream of Reformed scholars and Barthian 'Calvinists'. For my part, using the phrase "penal substitution" to assuage broader evangelicalism when we know we mean something completely different feels disingenuous. Indeed, I'm grateful that Wright clarified his position in The Day the Revolution Began where he forthrightly describes wrath-appeasement as paganizing the gospel.

"It's like saying, "I am a member of the Church of Jesus Christ of Latter-Day Saints" when I'm not a Mormon. The individual words of that phrase are true of me but the phrase of the whole has a history and carries its own meaning."

"*Even if there is a narrow sense in which Christ is said to be our substitute, it is more accurate to say his death is "for us" in the sense of 'for our benefit' rather than 'instead of' because he unites with us in death to die "AS us" and raises up humanity in his resurrection. And likewise, by faith we unite (identify) ourselves with him to both die and rise with him. In that union, there is an exchange of our poverty for His riches (2 Cor.8:9), our death for His life. So it's not so much about substitution as it is about union, identification and exchange. And even to say that Christ did for us what we could not do for ourselves is better described as a vicarious victory than a substitutionary penalty.*" (emphasis mine)[2]

DAVID BENTLEY HART

"But, even if it were found there, could one believe it? Why would one believe it? *I mean, it's a very strange belief, isn't it? That God is outraged at us for sins committed by someone else—that is a distant parent—even before we were born. That we also earn His outrage with sins we couldn't have avoided because we're corrupted by that distant fact [of "original sin"], and the way in which the*

"Loving God" has made it possible for some of us to be elected for forgiveness is through the violent murder of an innocent victim. This somehow satiates His wrath against sin.

*"[In the Bible] you're dealing with a different set of metaphors—*which are not false, they simply speak to us in the language of images because that's what we require—*in which the story of salvation is not this gambit, or game, or an act of substitutionary appeasement of irrational wrath. It's that the creatures that God loves have alienated themselves—His whole creation has been alienated from Him—and He enters into it at His own cost to rescue those He loves and goes all the way into the depths of utter estrangement—death and Hades—to effect that rescue."*

"If you go into the Eastern Orthodox Church today all you're going to hear about is the triumph over Death and the triumph over the powers that hold the Cosmos in thrall. Basically, the same Pauline language of the "powers and principalities on high being cast down" and "Christ taking captives" and "setting the prisoners free", etc.

"I guess it really does matter because if you're raised with an idea of the Atonement in the substitutionary sense, you have such a bizarrely-irrational and horrific picture of God fixed in your conscience that everything else flows from the dismal fact that this world seems to be the product of a psychotic omnipotent Deity." (emphasis mine)[3]

N.T. WRIGHT

"Clearly there have been distortions in what has been called "Penal Substitution Atonement." For me, I had quite a breakthrough in thinking about this some years ago, realizing the phrase 'penal substitution' can mean quite different things to different people,

according to which story you put it in. If you have an element of a story, and you frame it within one narrative, it means something quite different...*So, penal substitution can be expressed in very damaging ways. Even when preachers don't intend to do this. It is quite clearly the case that this is how many, many people—particularly young people—hear it. The idea being that there is this big, bullying, angry God who is very cross with us all and He's got a big stick and He's about to lash out and fortunately somebody gets in the way. It happens to be His own son, so that somehow makes it alright, and then we get off.*

"So, now, if that is what people have heard and are hearing, then we've got some serious work to do because we have taken John 3:16 which says "God so loved the world that He gave His only Son" and what people have heard is "God so hated the world that He killed His own Son."

"So we need to emphasize that what happens on the cross is the sovereign act of love on behalf of the Father Himself. The death of Jesus reveals the love of God as Paul says in Romans 5, "God commends His love to us in that while we were still sinners the Messiah died for us." For that you need a really tight nexus between God and Jesus because it makes no sense to say 'I love you so much but I'm sending somebody else to do the dirty work.'; [instead] 'I love you so much, I'm coming to do it myself.' So, there is a strong Trinitarian theology built into the New Testament at that very point."

"In the New Testament, the results of the death of Jesus isn't simply that I was very sinful and now fortunately somebody has taken my punishment so I get to go to Heaven. To say that is actually to moralize our vision of what it means to be human." (emphasis mine)

RICHARD ROHR

"Many rightly or wrongly wondered, "What will God ask of me if God demands violent blood sacrifice from his only Son?" Particularly if they had a rageaholic or abusive parent, they were already programmed to believe in punishment as the shape of the universe. A violent theory of redemption legitimated punitive and violent problem solving all the way down--from papacy to parenting. There eventually emerged a disconnect between the founding story of necessary punishment and Jesus' message. If God uses and needs violence to attain God's purposes, maybe Jesus did not really mean what he said in the Sermon on the Mount (Matthew 5), and violent means are really good and necessary."[4]

JAMES D.G. DUNN

"... "expiation" does seem to be the better translation [than "propitiation"] for Rom. 3:25. The fact is that for Paul God is the subject of the action; it is God who provided Jesus as a [hilasterion]. And if God is the subject, then the obvious object is sin or the sinner. To argue that God provided Jesus as a means of propitiating God is certainly possible, but less likely I think. For one thing, regularly in the Old Testament the immediate object of the action denoted by the Hebrew kipper is the removal of sin—either by purifying the person or object, or by wiping out the sin; the act of atonement "cancels", "purges away" sin. It is not God who is the object of this atonement, nor the wrath of God, but the sin which calls forth the wrath of God." (emphasis mine)[5]

JEFFREY JOHN

"As he said, "Whoever sees me has seen the Father". Jesus is what God is. He is the one who shows us God's nature. And the most basic truth about God's nature is that he is love, not wrath and punishment.' [8.07-08.21 min.]; 'The cross, then, is not about Jesus reconciling an angry God to us; it's almost the opposite. It's about a totally loving God, incarnate in Christ, reconciling us to him. *On the cross, Jesus dies for our sins, the price of sin is paid, but it's not paid to God, but by God.* As St Paul says ... *Because he is love, God does what love does: unites himself with the beloved. He enters his own creation and goes to the bottom line for us. Not sending a substitute to vent his punishment on, but going himself to the bitter end, sharing in the worst of suffering and grief that life can throw at us, and finally sharing our death so that he can bring us through death to eternal life in him.'* [09.37-10.36 min.]; '...so far from inflicting suffering and punishment, be bears our griefs and shares our sorrow. From Good Friday on, God is no longer God up there, inscrutably allotting rewards and retributions; on the cross, even more than in the crib, he is Emmanuel, God down here, God with us." (emphasis mine)[6]

JONATHAN WYNNE-JONES

"In other words, Jesus took the rap and we got forgiven as long as we said we believed in him…This is repulsive as well as nonsensical. It makes God sound like a psychopath. If a human behaved like this we'd say that they were a monster."[7]

JOHN CALVIN

"Now, we see that all those who know not God know not themselves; because they have God present with them not only in the excellent gifts of the mind, but in their very essence; because it belongeth to God alone to be, all other things have their being in him. Also, we learn out of this place that God did not so create the world once that he did afterward depart from his work; but that it standeth by his power..."[8]

ENDNOTES

INTRODUCTION

1. C.S. Lewis, *Mere Christianity*, pg. 57–58

2. See Hebrews 12:28; James 2:5; 2 Peter 1:11; Revelation 1:6; 1:9; 5:10; 11:15; 12:10

CHAPTER 1

1. William Barclay, *Crucified and Crowned* (S.C.M, first published 1961), pg. 100

2. Paul R. Eddy and James Beilby, 'The Atonement: An Introduction', in P. R. Eddy and J. Beilby, editors, *The Nature of the Atonement: Four Views*; Downers Grove: IVP, 2006, pg. 12

3. J. Denny Weaver (2001), *The Nonviolent Atonement*, Wm. B. Eerdmans Publishing, pg. 18

4. Ibid

5. Wayne Grudem, *Systematic Theology: An Introduction to Biblical Doctrine*, pg. 539

6. Michael Green, *The Empty Cross of Jesus* (Eastbourne: Kingsway, 2004; first published 1984), pgs. 64–65

7. H. N. Oxenham, *The Catholic Doctrine Of The Atonement* (London: Longman, Green, Longman, Roberts, and Green, 1865), pg. 119

8. See 7 Theories of the Atonement Summarized by Stephen D. Morrison, https://www.sdmorrison.org/7-theories-of-the-atonement-summarized/

9. Paul R. Eddy and James Beilby, 'The Atonement: An Introduction', in P. R. Eddy and J. Beilby, editors, *The Nature of the Atonement: Four Views*; Downers Grove: IVP, 2006, pg. 12

10. Brad Jersak, *A More Christlike God*, pg.229

11. 'The Atonement: An Introduction', in P. R. Eddy and J. Beilby [eds], *The Nature of the Atonement: Four Views* [Downers Grove: IVP, 2006], pg. 17

12. H. N. Oxenham, *The Catholic Doctrine Of The Atonement* (London: Longman, Green, Longman, Roberts, and Green, 1865), pg. 119

13. While this verse starts off by God saying "I am not rebuking you for your sacrifices", this appears in context to be an acknowledgement that the people have done a good job following the command to offer animal sacrifices. So, God's complaint is not that they have failed to do this. His complaint is that He does not have any need for these animal sacrifices, as made clear in the following verses. As with Jeremiah 7:21–23 above, the sacrificial system is dismissed in favor of a call to practice obedience to God in the heart and to offer praise and thanksgiving rather than blood sacrifices.

14. H. N. Oxenham, *The Catholic Doctrine Of The Atonement* (London: Longman, Green, Longman, Roberts, and Green, 1865), pgs. 112–113.

15. Karl Barth, *Church Dogmatics IV*, pg. 253

16. C.S. Lewis, *Mere Christianity*, pg. 59

17. Also quoted from my book "Jesus Undefeated: Condemning the False Doctrine of Eternal Torment", pg. 147-149

18. From the video "4 Questions For David Bentley Hart" hosted by Keith Giles, August 18, 2020: https://www.patreon.com/posts/4-questions-for-40602314

19. This is also something I cover in greater detail in chapter 2 of my book, *Jesus Untangled: Crucifying Our Politics To Pledge Allegiance To The Lamb*.

20. As quoted from my book, *Jesus Unexpected: Ending the End Times To Become The Second Coming*, pgs. 147–148.

21. As quoted in my book, *Jesus Undefeated: Condemning the False Doctrine of Eternal Torment*, pgs. 153–154

22. Quoted from "Unwrathing God: Nonviolent atonement, eschatology & practice", Bradley Jersak, YouTube, Sept. 12, 2020, https://www.youtube.com/watch?v=1OFIoZpcbjM

23. Lyonett, Stanislas (1973). "Expiation". In Léon-Dufour, Xavier (ed.). *Dictionary of Biblical Theology [Vocabulaire de theologie biblique]* (2nd, revised ed.). London: Geoffrey Chapman. pg. 156.

CHAPTER 2

1. Brad Jersak, *A More Christlike God*, pg. 261

2. Marcus Borg, "Christianity Divided by the Cross," October 25, 2013, http://www.patheos.com/blogs/marcusborg/2013/10/christianity-divided-by-the-cross/

3. Marcus Borg, "The Real Meanings of the Cross," October 28, 2013, http://www.patheos.com/blogs/marcusborg/2013/10/the-real-meanings-of-the-cross/

4. Richard Rohr, "Substitutionary Atonement," Sunday, July 23, 2017, https://cac.org/substitutionary-atonement-2017-07-23/

5. Marcus Borg, "Christianity Divided by the Cross," October 25, 2013, http://www.patheos.com/blogs/marcusborg/2013/10/christianity-divided-by-the-cross/

6. Richard Rohr, "A Nonviolent Atonement," Monday, July 24, 2017, https://cac.org/a-nonviolent-atonement-2017-07-24/

7. Brad Jersak, *A More Christlike God*, pg. 261

CHAPTER 3

1. From "Do you believe in penal substitution? // Ask NT Wright Anything," YouTube, Dec. 3, 2018, https://www.youtube.com/watch?v=pkXI33hpe2o

2. From *The Mediation of Christ*, C. Baxter Kruger, 2020, pg.12. Available as a free PDF download at https://perichoresis.org/pages/the-mediation-of-jesus-christ

3. Everett Ferguson, *The Church of Christ: A Biblical Ecclesiology for Today* (Grand Rapids: Eerdmans, 1996), pgs. 150–152

4.   Brad Jersak, from a personal email correspondence, Sept. 18, 2020.

5.   From *The Mediation of Christ*, C. Baxter Kruger, 2020, pg. 20. Available as a free PDF download at https://perichoresis.org/pages/the-mediation-of-jesus-christ

CHAPTER 4

1.   David Bentley Hart, *The Doors of the Sea: Where Was God In The Tsunami?*, pgs. 86–87

2.   For more on this concept of how Jesus redefines God's Holiness in contrast to the Pharisees, see the book, *Jesus, A New Vision,* by Marcus Borg.

3.   From "Do you believe in penal substitution? // Ask NT Wright Anything," YouTube, Dec. 3, 2018, https://www.youtube.com/watch?v=pkXI33hpe2o

CHAPTER 5

1.   Marlene Winell, *Leaving The Fold* (Oakland, Ca: New Harbinger, 1993), pg. 1

2.   Quoted in Richard Marius, *Martin Luther: The Christian Between God and Death*, Harvard University Press, 2000, p. 20; primary source, TR 5, no. 5537—footnote on pg. 491.

3.   Note: Some people may struggle with emotional disorders, clinical depression or even mental illnesses that make it much more challenging to deal with feelings of worthlessness. If you struggle with these feelings and thoughts, you may consider seeking out a licensed therapist or psychologist who can help you overcome these challenges.

CHAPTER 6

1.   O.C. Quick, *Doctrines of the Creed,* Scribner's, 1938, pg. 232

2.   Rene Girard, *I See Satan Fall Like Lightning*, Orbis Books, 2001, pg. 9

3.   Ibid, pg. 10

4.   Ibid, pg. 11

5. Ibid, pgs. 11–12

6. From a private email conversation on this topic, Sept. 24, 2020

7. Ibid, pg. 13–14

8. Ibid, pg. 56

9. Ibid, pg. 26

10. Ibid, pg. 65

11. Ibid, pg. 191

12. Ibid, pg. 143

CHAPTER 7

1. Edward J. Kilmartin, *The Eucharist in the West, History and Theology*, Collegeville, MN: Liturgical Press, 1999. pg. 381

2. From the video interview, "Why Did Jesus [Have To] Die?", Bruxy Cavey and Keith Giles, Sept. 1, 2020: https://www.patreon.com/posts/bruxy-cavey-and-41129220

3. Ibid

4. *The Mediation Of Christ*, C. Baxter Kruger, pg. 17

5. From the video interview, "Why Did Jesus [Have To] Die?", Bruxy Cavey and Keith Giles, Sept. 1, 2020

6. Ibid

CHAPTER 8

1. J.F. Bethune-Baker, *An Introduction to the Early History of Christian Doctrine to the Time of the Council of Chalcedon* (London: Methuen & Co, 1903), pgs. 328 and 351–352

2. From the video interview, "Why Did Jesus [Have To] Die?", Bruxy Cavey and Keith Giles, Sept. 1, 2020: https://www.patreon.com/posts/bruxy-cavey-and-41129220

3. From "Richard Rohr's Daily Meditation", Friday, Feb. 12, 2016. Incarnation instead of Atonement: https://myemail.constantcontact.

com/Richard-Rohr-s-Meditation--Incarnation-instead-of-Atonement.
html?soid=1103098668616&aid=6eQ87B8yCnY

4.   Richard Rohr, "Salvation As At-One-Ment," Daily
Devotional, Tues. July 25, 2017, https://cac.org/
incarnation-instead-atonement-2017-07-25/

5.   David Bentley Hart on Penal Substitutionary Atonement,
YouTube Video, Sept. 26, 2019, https://www.youtube.com/
watch?v=ioNI8kQydwE

6.   Brad Jersak, *A More Christlike God*, pgs. 256–257

7.   See Plato's *Republic*, Book II, pgs. 360–361

8.   Rene Girard, *I See Satan Fall Like Lightning*, pg. 191

CHAPTER 9

1.   C. Baxter Kruger, *The Mediation of Christ*, pgs. 12–13

2.   From David Bentley Hart, *The Experience of God*, pg. 8

APPENDIX

1.   From "Do you believe in penal substitution? // Ask NT Wright
Anything," YouTube, Dec. 3, 2018, https://www.youtube.com/
watch?v=pkXI33hpe2o

2.   Brad Jersak from a personal email 9/18/2020

3.   David Bentley Hart on Penal Substitutionary Atonement,
YouTube Video, Sept. 26, 2019, https://www.youtube.com/
watch?v=ioNI8kQydwE

4.   From "Richard Rohr's Daily Meditation", Friday, Feb. 12, 2016.
Incarnation instead of Atonement: https://myemail.constantcontact.
com/Richard-Rohr-s-Meditation--Incarnation-instead-of-Atonement.
html?soid=1103098668616&aid=6eQ87B8yCnY

5.   James D.G. Dunn, "Paul's Understanding of the Death of Jesus" in
Robert Banks (ed.), *Reconciliation and Hope* (Carlisle: Paternoster Press,
1974), pg. 137

6. Jeffrey John, Lent Talks, BBC Radio 4 on 04/04/07, at 13.22–13.45 min

7. Jonathan Wynne-Jones, "Easter message: Christ did not die for sin" in The Telegraph, 01/04/07. Online (accessed 27/02/11)

8. John Calvin, *Commentary on Acts,* 17:28

For more information about Keith Giles
or to contact him for speaking engagements,
please visit *www.KeithGiles.com*

Many voices. One message.

Quoir is a boutique publisher
with a singular message: *Christ is all.*
Venture beyond your boundaries to discover Christ
in ways you never thought possible.

For more information, please visit
www.quoir.com

HERETIC HAPPY HOUR

Burning questions, not people.

Heretic Happy Hour is an unapologetically irreverent, crass, and sometimes profound conversation about the Christian faith. Hosts, Keith Giles, Katy Valentine, Derrick Day, and Matthew Distefano pull no punches and leave no stones unturned. For some serious sacred cow-tipping, there's nothing better than spending an hour of your time with us.

www.heretichappyhour.com

CPSIA information can be obtained
at www.ICGtesting.com
Printed in the USA
LVHW101200241021
701269LV00005B/44